The Murder Stone

P.K. Kaplan

Publisher:
ASPG (Australian Self Publishing Group)
P.O. Box 159, Calwell, ACT Australia 2905
Email: publishaspg@gmail.com
http://www.inspiringpublishers.com

National Library of Australia Cataloguing-in-Publication entry

Author: P.K. Kaplan

Title: **The Murder Stone**/*P.K. Kaplan*

ISBN: 978-1-922920-90-4 (Print)

ISBN: 978-1-922920-91-1 (ePub2)

ISBN: 978-1-922920-92-8 (PDF eBook)

To Terrence and Albert.

A story from Nana's head.

✧

1

Joe had barely stepped outside when he could feel the humidity clinging to him like a wet towel. The weather up here was a bugger at this time of the year. When it wasn't raining, it felt as though it was raining. Damn Innisfail. At times like this he wondered how the hell he'd managed to end up this far north. It wasn't his country. He was from the south coast where you had a proper dry summer and wet winter, so he was glad to be leaving - even if where he was heading wouldn't be much better.

He loaded the last of his things into his old truck, then put the keys of the flat into an envelope and shoved them through the mail slot, just as the landlord had asked him to. Then he was gone.

Dusk is a bad time to be on the road up here, but when your truck has no air conditioning a long trip during the heat of the day can wipe you out. Anyway he was used to traveling at night. He liked the feeling of being a solitary traveler through the darkness. The shortest route would be to drive south a bit and connect to the Flinders Highway and then straight on to Hughenden, then to Cloncurry, but he'd decided to take the backroads through the tablelands until he reached the Palmerston Highway. It's a difficult road that winds all the way up the mountains, with some tricky hairpin bends. Then when you finally reach the top, it winds all the way down again.

Adding to the danger, it's barely two lanes wide and what little light the moon offers is often blacked out by the thick canopy of trees. But once he'd negotiated that, he'd turn onto the Kennedy Highway for the rest of the journey to Hugheden. All in all it would probably add a couple of hours to the trip, but what the heck, it would be a bit of an adventure and his truck had good brakes - he'd checked them himself that morning.

Joe shoved his favorite CD into the slot and turned up the sound. *'The best of Hunters and Collectors.'* The CD player was one of the reasons he hadn't traded up for a newer truck. He wasn't into downloading and streaming.

He was barely out of town when nightfall turned the entire landscape into a featureless scene of blackness. The rainforest was getting denser and encroaching closer and closer to the edge of the road. He could feel the air outside cooling and getting drier as he went up and up, and he wound down his windows to let it soak into his cabin. Now the twists and turns were so close together that even on high-beam he could see only a short distance ahead. He stopped singing along to his CD, gripped the steering wheel and concentrated on each curve, keeping careful watch for any headlights ahead that would signal an on-coming car. He was on the dangerous side where the road dropped away to nothing, and the last thing he needed was to find himself suddenly having to swerve to miss another crazy person like himself, driving though here at night.

Finally, he reached the safety of the flat lands and turned onto the Kennedy Highway. 'Highway' might be overstating it a little. It was barely two lanes wide and mostly still unsealed. Promises had been made and it was certainly looking better than the last time he was through here, but its former name 'Kennedy Development Road' was maybe a more accurate description.

The Oasis Roadhouse at The Lynd, was a legendary stop not just for locals, but for gray nomads with their mobile homes and caravans and 4WD adventurers. The Oasis itself was little more than a truck stop really, with a camping ground, a few motel units, and a pub that seemed to have become a 'must see' attraction for everyone traveling through the area. Tonight it was packed out. Twenty or so cars out the front, caravans out the back and music blaring. Unusual for a weeknight. It was tempting to pop in for a quick one but he needed to keep sharp so he only stopped long enough to top up his petrol.

Just a few kilometers down the road at Lyndhurst, there was nothing. Just a faint light hanging over the 'Petrol & Tyres" sign. No cars either. In fact he hadn't seen a single vehicle since he left The Oasis. He pulled over, took a piss in the bush and poured a coffee from his thermos. It was just after 10pm. Plenty of time to make it to the Hughenden Caravan Park before midnight. He hoped the cafe next door to the park was still there. He was looking forward to a good breakfast before going on to Cloncurry and they did a fantastic bacon and egg sandwich.

Over at the truckstop, a raggedy stack of tyres was caged like wild animals. On the front was a sign that said **Ring the bell for help.** But there was no sign of a bell.

After a few minutes walking around to stretch his legs, Joe set off again. Still no cars, but some fresh roadkill on the side of the road. Somebody must have been through recently, the dogs hadn't gotten to it yet.

He flicked his lights to high-beam to see further ahead and in his rear mirror, caught sight of headlights approaching from behind. It was on an unsealed section of the road, and it was throwing up clouds of dust. He must have been going at a hell of a pace, because Joe was doing over 100 and this guy was gaining on him quickly. Then just as suddenly, the car turned off to his left and was gone.

He was now only about 20 km from Hughenden, but the road around here was pretty rough so you had to keep an eye out for various road hazards. Up ahead, his headlights seemed to be picking up something on the shoulder of the road.. Maybe a small Roo. He slowed right down as he went past it. "Shit, it's a body."

He backed up so that his headlights could give him a better look. A woman - young, well dressed, laying face down with her head turned to the right. Her arms were raised above her head, palms down, like she'd been saying to her attacker 'don't shoot.' But there was no obvious sign she had been shot. The one eye he could see was wide open. No sign of blood on her body, but some dark areas near her head could be blood that had soaked into the earth. Her pants were down around her ankles and her shoes were missing - but her feet were clean, so she hadn't walked there.

Joe knew better than to touch her. He picked up a stick and poked at her arm. It was already pretty stiff. He looked around for a car that might have been hers but couldn't see anything. Then he checked his phone. "Bugger" - there was no phone reception out here - he'd have to drive into Hughenden for help. Just in case another car did come along, he took two emergency road safety signs from the back of his truck and placed one at each end of her body. Then as an afterthought, he taped a note on one of them that said. **'Don't touch!! Have gone to Hughenden for help.'** He wasn't very confident people would look at the note first, but he left it there anyway.

A few kilometers down the road his phone came to life with a jolt. He pulled over and called the local police. A woman who identified herself as Senior Constable Forde answered the phone. She took down the details and asked Joe to go back to the body and wait for the police to arrive. About half an hour later, three vehicles came racing up the road towards him. The first, with lights flashing, was a police car driven by a uniformed policewoman who Joe presumed was the constable he had spoken to - and with a much older man - clearly her senior in the passenger's seat. The second was a dark coloured official-looking van- presumedly for removing the body, and the third a fancy 4WD, driven by a man who appeared to have been woken from a deep sleep and was wearing shorts, an old Brisbane Broncos T shirt and thongs. He - it turned out - was the local doctor.

Senior Sergeant Jack Harding introduced himself and Senior Constable Forde to Joe before heading straight over to the body where the doctor was trying to determine what had happened. After making some initial examinations and taking numerous photos, he turned the woman's body over. There was a kind of collective sucking in of breath as they saw what remained of her face. The left side of her head had been totally smashed in - but not here. There was not enough blood or tissue on the ground and it appeared the damage had been done some time before she'd been left there. Maybe a couple of hours even. Disappointingly, there were few clues as to how she got there. No fresh tyre tracks visible except for Joes, no drag marks to indicate the direction she might have come from, no murder weapon. Nothing.

No one knew who she was either. Not the doctor. Not the police. And nothing on her body or clothes gave any clue as to who she was. There was no phone or purse - although maybe a complete search of the area in the light of day might throw up something.

Dr Adam Sidowski clearly felt the situation was beyond his level of expertise, other than estimating she had been dead for at least 3 hours. He was a family doctor - which meant he did see a bit of family violence, but this was at another level. He wanted the police to bring in a pathologist from Mt Isa and a forensics team. There were too many things about the scene that he just didn't feel comfortable commenting on. After a number of phone calls, it was agreed the body would be placed in the coolroom of a local funeral home until the morning and the site would be sealed off until a forensics team could come across from Mt Isa. Joe, who knew even less about what had happened here than the doctor or police, would be required to give a complete account of where he'd been, where he was going and what he knew about the death. He was, as Senior Sergeant Harding kept reminding him, "just a witness mate." but Joe knew there was more to it than that. He was a proud Yuin Yuin man and he knew that it didn't matter where you were, if you were at the scene of the crime, you were a suspect. Besides, he'd heard many times that old bit of police folklore that says that the person who calls in the crime is often the perpetrator.

By the time he got back to the station to make his formal statement, it was 3am. His request to get some sleep and come by in the morning was refused. He was however offered coffee and breakfast - not as good as the one he had been looking forward to.

By 6am, he'd given his statement, had his fingerprints taken (to rule him out), given a DNA sample (also, he was assured, to rule him out) and given assurances that once he arrived in Cloncurry he would make himself known to the local police just in case they had any further questions. Then he headed to the caravan park, picked up the keys to site 15B and quickly fell asleep.

Meanwhile, Hughenden had become like a crime film set. The town hadn't experienced anything like this since the old days when it was a wild mining town. The mood was a mixture of horror and prurient interest. Everyone involved in the actual case was keen to do everything by the book. Dr Sidowski had made meticulous notes, taken all sorts of measurements and taken numerous photos from every possible angle. And the police were keen to wrap the case up quickly to show that rural police are just as competent as their city mates, despite having less back-up. It was maybe not the best case to try and demonstrate their capabilities. After all, they didn't even know who the victim was, so there weren't any logical suspects.

First to arrive at the Funeral Home - rather dramatically by helicopter - was the eminent pathologist, Professor Peter Castleton. He was one of the nations most respected pathologists and had chosen to work in Mt Isa rather than in a major city so that he could pursue his special interest - native plants and insects and their medicinal properties. He had written an authoritative book on the subject which had generated a great deal of interest from various pharmaceutical companies and was often invited to address international forums on plant medicine.

Under normal circumstances, a straightforward post mortem of a murder victim wouldn't have warranted the involvement of someone as highly qualified as the Professor, but as it happened, he had been supervising a post mortem of a quite bizarre murder victim in Cloncurry on the previous day, and he was more than happy to help.

Both the police and Dr Sidowski were particularly pleased to have him on the team, as a gruesome murder such as this would probably make the news all over Australia and maybe even gain international attention. The sooner it was cleared up the better.

After a brief examination and a look over Dr Sidowski's notes which he seemed impressed with, the Professor arranged for the body to be flown to Mt Isa immediately.

The forensic team arrived in Hughenden soon after and quickly went to work at the site. Within hours they'd found what looked like 'disguised footprints' leading to car tracks. The tracks were pretty messy because the car had driven out the same way it had driven in and carefully gone over the tracks. They had also found what appeared to be a small amount of human tissue near the tyre tracks and on the ground near to where the body was found. But there were no signs of a weapon, scraps of paper, cigarette butts, or anything else that might help. No sign of the missing shoes either, or of her belongings. The crime scene photographs showed a body that had been placed awkwardly, as though it had been posed before rigor had completely set in, but somehow not sitting quite right on the road. Perhaps she'd been laying in that position somewhere else - then moved here. Hopefully Professor Castleton could shed some light on the matter. Meanwhile there was the matter of her identification.

By the end of the day, Professor Castleton had issued an interim report that noted *the body being placed on a hot dirt and bitumen road on a cool night has complicated the time of death estimate somewhat by affecting the core body temperature.* However he agreed with Dr Sidowski that 'the victim was killed between 6pm and 8pm and that the body had been on the road 'two or three hours at most.' Cause of death was obviously blunt force trauma which all but destroyed the left hand side of her brain and there were no defensive wounds or signs of a struggle, which he noted, 'is *a bit of a surprise, given that the female victim is a young strapping woman of slightly taller than average height'.*

The report put her age at 'between 30-35, otherwise healthy, never given birth, no tattoos or other distinctive marks and no sign of recent sexual activity or trauma. The female victim's teeth were all in good order so dental records may help in identification. There were no grass seeds or foreign materials on her clothing or in the nasal cavities. *'When taking the victim's fingerprints to assist identification, I noticed a sticky substance under one fingernail, so I took a swab for testing And of course we will run a complete set of blood tests to see if that explains the lack of defensive wounds. But the victim had not consumed any alcohol recently and there was no sign of drug use. The stomach contents also suggested she had not eaten for several hours prior to her death and that her last meal was most likely a hamburger.'*

Professor Castleton had also produced a DNA profile 'just in case she's on a data bank' and done a quick blood match in case it might be needed to help identification - 'Type O positive. Too common to be much help.'

By now the police had carried out a complete check of missing persons from NSW and Queensland that fitted the age and description of the woman, but found nothing. - Not a total surprise because she may not have been missing long enough yet for anyone to have noticed. But just in case, they had a police artist recreate an image of what the woman might look like had her face not been caved in, ready to release to the press.

While they waited for answers Jack Harding decided to head over to Manoora and see if anyone there knew her.

Manoora was basically a fly-in, fly-out mining town that lived on the scraps left over from the gold boom. The mine had the impressive name of *Wolfram Bowenfield* which disguised the fact that it was always on the verge of bankruptcy. Besides the mine and a bunch of prefab houses that had been trucked in, there was a small single storey pub, a general store with a petrol bowser out the front, two motels and a general mechanical repair place that claimed it could fix just about anything. In any place that has a temporary workforce of men that far outnumber women, sex workers are always in demand. But the mining company was keen to stress that the miners lived in a hostel next to the mine - and the only women allowed in were those who worked there. The rule was strictly enforced - but all that meant was that over the years the sex workers had gradually turned the more run-down of the two motels into an unofficial brothel. Everyone in town - especially the motel's owners, just turned a blind eye. You'd have to be desperate to work there, and most of the women were. They were all running away from something. Drugs, debts, violence, the law - or all of the above. Even so, they rarely hung around for long. Most just passed through, staying a few weeks or months then heading out. There was always the possibility our victim was one of them, although neither Dr Sidowski or Professor Castleton thought so. She was too healthy, too clean and too well dressed. Still someone there might know her.

Manoora was no help. No one had seen anyone who looked remotely like her. As the publican said, "does she look like she'd hang around in a place like this?"

A week went by. The toxicology tests came back negative. Just healthy blood that was a bit low on vitamin D. Her fingerprints were not on file and no new missing persons reports had been filed.

The swabs taken from the substance under her fingernail revealed the presence of minute traces of cellulose gum. Professor Castleton seemed surprised but pointed out that it is used in food processing as a thickener - so maybe we should be investigating food processing plants in the region. Unfortunately, there were none.

Then suddenly, a few days later, out of the blue came a request from the police in Albury of all places. A hire car company had reported that a Nissan X-trail hire car rented 12 days ago hadn't been returned. The woman who'd rented the car had mentioned that she wanted to visit her elderly grandfather in Mt Isa and that her little hatchback might not be up to the task. She would return the car in 7 days. The car was now well overdue and the woman had not contacted them. Meanwhile, they had been trying to contact her, but her phone was either turned off or out of range. Assuming the car was now stolen, or involved in an accident some-where, they contacted the police who called around to her home address but found nobody at home. The police had also checked her workplace only to find that the company records showed she had taken 10 days leave for family rea-sons and had been due back at work the previous day but had not turned up. Several workmates mentioned that she had received news that her grandfather was close to death so she'd taken leave pretty suddenly - they assumed she was late back from holidays because he had died. No one had any idea what her grandfather's name was, or where he lived - other than Mt Isa - and there was no record that she had signed in as a visitor to any of the town's aged care homes. As she was now considered missing and the hire car had been reported as stolen, Albury police had sent through a photo of her license to every station in the area with a request to look out for her.

So now they knew the identity of the murder victim.

Adele Farmer, 32, unmarried, marketing executive at a food production company specializing in frozen desserts. Moved to Albury just over a year ago. Got on well with her workmates. No boyfriend that anyone knew of. Most of her family lived in Sydney, but they weren't the kind of family that kept tabs on one another, which is probably why no one had noticed she was missing.

Her mother had mentioned to her some time ago that her grandfather - who she had always been close to as a child, was close to death. A few weeks ago, Adele had mentioned to her mother that she would try to get some time off from work to visit him but she hadn't phoned to confirm she was going.

She never arrived at her grandfather's house but he wouldn't have known anyway because he died the day after she left to visit him.

Finding out the identity of the victim was one thing, but where was her car? There was no sign of it around the area where she had been found, and despite an extensive search up the highway from Albury to Cloncurry and across to Hughenden it still hadn't been found. Nor could the police understand how she'd ended up in Hughenden - around 4 hours drive from Cloncurry and way off the route to Mt Isa.

Her family had been relieved to hear that she hadn't at least been raped, despite the partially removed panties, but that was just another part of the mystery. It was almost as though she'd been attacked as she was starting to undress - maybe in a public toilet somewhere, or maybe she'd pulled off the road somewhere to relieve herself in the bush and been attacked there and dragged into her attacker's car and taken to Hughenden. But why would that be? Everyone had a theory, but none of them made much sense. The most frustrating thing for investigators was the complete lack of evidence. It was as though her body had been wiped clean. Even her clothes - which looked freshly laundered - gave up no clues. Until they found the car, or the murder weapon, or something new turned up on security camera footage from around Cloncurry or Hughenden, they were at a dead end.

✦

2

Six months later, Senior Sergeant Harding turned up at the cattle station where Joe was working. The Mitchelton family who owned the property had hired him to help replace the boundary fencing damaged by local flooding and rebuild a farm shed that had been destroyed when a generator blew up. Joe was a carpenter by trade - but like most tradies he could turn his hand to fixing anything, and Dave Mitchelton had kept him on to help around the place. 'The wife wants him to do some renovations to smarten up the place.. She's wanted a new kitchen for years.' He had found Joe to be a good worker, sober...'no trouble, just gets on with the job' and had from day 1, never believed he had anything to do with the murder.

Having assured Dave that Joe wasn't in any trouble, Jack took a cooler from his car and walked over to the verandah where Joe was waiting.

"Want a drink? I've got beer or soft drink"

'I have a choice?'

'You do..I don't..... I had a bit of a run in with the grog a few years ago, so I'm strictly on the soft stuff now.'

'Bad place to be a policeman if you can't have a drink.'

'It was tough for a while. Everyone was waiting for me to fall off the wagon - even my wife. But it's all good now.'

Joe helped himself to a beer.

'So why are you here?'

'It's about that woman you found. Adele Palmer. We're really struggling with this one. No clues, haven't found the car. And the last place she was actually seen - positively identified on security footage, was on the day before she was found - filling up with petrol in Broken Hill. After that nothing. The NSW police are looking at the case too - Mt Isa police are also still investigating and my Senior Constable - Forde, you remember her? - has made it an out-of- hours hobby to find out how Adele ended up here. She's drawn up a whole lot of charts and time lines and is convinced the body had only been dumped a short time before you found it. The pathologist fella - Castleton, he put it at a couple of hours, but she reckons he might have left just minutes before.

So here's what I'm wondering. Did you see or hear anything, anything at all that could indicate someone else was there when you pulled up?'

Joe closed his eyes and tried to recreate the scene in his head. He had done this many times to try and come to grips with the shock of it but it was always the same. Blackness except for the light of his headlights, silence except for the car's engine and the crunch of the gravel under his boots.

"I could see that she was laid out too neat for it to have been a hit and run. Like she'd been just put there. That really freaked me out. I didn't want to touch her or anything. But I've told you all this before.'

Jack had been hoping for something more. A feeling, a shadow, something.

"You were freaked out and yet you had the presence of mind not to touch her....Why?.....Are you sure you didn't - I dont know - sense something?"

Joe tipped out the rest of his beer and crushed the can.

"Nothing like that....it's just...I've got a brother, Kev. Always been in trouble with the cops. Nothing serious. Caught joyriding once or twice when he was 13 or 14. A bit of weed, drunk and disorderly. Anyway one night he ends up at a party at this big, fancy house. It had a pool and everything. Everyone is out of it - including Kev. It's getting messy, the neighbours are upset and they call the police. He's the only blackfella there so he legs it. But he has no idea where he is. He's walking around for a while looking for a road he recognizes or a sign that will tell him where he is but it's all just respectable middle class homes with nice front gardens. Suddenly he hears this 'bang'. A guy wearing some sort of mask runs out of the house, flings something in the garden, jumps into the passenger side of an old Ford and they take off. Kev - still out of it - walks over to see what the guy dropped, hoping it's money or something he can sell. It's a gun. Stupidly he picks it up and looks at it. Then he catches on to what has happened, drops the gun and starts to run. Meanwhile some neighbours who had come out to see what was going on saw him drop the gun and run. When the police arrive the neighbours give them a pretty good description of my brother - 'he's an Abo.' - So now, they have the gun with his prints - and because he still has no idea where he is, they soon pick him up. The couple inside the house are jewellers and both have been shot dead. Well the husband survives for a few days - but then he's dead.

Kev tells them his side of the story but he has two problems. First, nobody at the party is going to come forward and swear he was there, because most of them have their own issues with the police. And then there's the car. He describes the make, model and colour - metallic gold. But as it turns out, Ford didn't make those cars in metallic gold. Now my brother is not that bright, but if there's one thing he does know - it's cars. He knew it had been customized, but nobody was interested in looking into that. They thought he was just making it up. Of course they could tell right off he wasn't the ringleader- it was pretty obvious he knew nothing about gemstones....nothing. So they offered to go easier on him if he gave up the names. Yeah right. What could he say? Anyway for the cops, it was a pretty open and shut case. They had the gun with only his prints on it - the other guy must have been smart enough to wear gloves. They had the witness who saw him with the gun in his hand.... and he had no explanation for why he was there at that time of night. Or at least none that any of his so-called mates would back up. The jury came back with guilty in less than an hour. .....'

Joe took a deep breath and continued.

'Anyway he did 5 years before the gold metallic car turned up following a botched armed robbery and a messy car chase. It rolled a couple of times and ended up smashed into a brick wall. The driver was killed instantly but it turned out he and his brother had done time for robbery before. And the younger brother was also in a relationship with the receptionist who worked in the jewellery place owned by the couple who were killed. Even then it took another few months to get his conviction overturned........ So you see, I know better than to touch anything at a crime scene.'

'So where's your brother now?'

"Back in jail mate. Got 18 months for dealing meth with one of his cell mates.'

Jack packed up his esky, wished Joe well and headed back to Hughenden. Nothing more to be learned here. Nina Forde would be disappointed though.

A year passed and still there was no new evidence. There'd been an inquest that found Adele had been murdered by a person or persons unknown but with no known motive There was nothing in the report to lead investigators to a suspect. Nina Forde would still visit the site regularly hoping to find something that no one had seen before and Adele's family had visited, said some prayers and laid some flowers on the exact spot where she'd been found - but that was it. The people of Hughenden had decided it wasn't one of them who did it and got on with life. Occasionally an abandoned car that vaguely fitted the description of the hire car would be reported somewhere and there'd be a flurry of activity at whichever police station was closest - but it was never the one. Any hope Jack and his team had that they were going to wrap this one up quickly had turned into dust.

$\diamondsuit$

3

Jack Harding had just finished a whole lot of paperwork and was about to head home early. It was his wife's birthday.

The phone call that came through hit him in the gut so hard he wanted to throw up. It was from a police station in Cloncurry - and it was about a missing person. Amy Moreno, aged 37. Supposed to arrive 4 days ago to work as a beauty therapist at the "Hair and Now" hair and beauty salon. She hadn't arrived and wasn't answering her phone. All that was known is that she had definitely left Brisbane 7 days ago, planned to drive up the coast to spend a day or two in Townsville and drive inland to Cloncurry. She was looking forward to her new job and talked about buying a share of the business if it all worked out. If she took the route she planned, she would have passed through Hughenden. They would email through a recent photo and details of her car. 'Could you ask around?' The caller didn't add - but he could have - 'especially as you have already had one body there.'

Amy Moreno looked younger than her 37 years - but it was a photo from her beauty business website so who knew how accurate it was. Jack realized his hand was shaking as he picked up the copies of the photo from the printer.

Not a word had passed between Jack and Nina but she'd heard the call. "How long do you reckon before we find the body?"

'Nah, you're jumping the gun a bit. We'll get onto it in the morning.'

He left the copies of her photo on his desk and went home.

Nobody recognized Amy. Not here, not all the way back to Prairie, or south to Tangorin. And just to be certain - Manoora was canvassed too, although she had no reason to be there. She'd just disappeared without trace. They had a little more luck with the car. A small white Kia stood out a bit here where SUVs and trucks were more the go. A couple of people in Burra sort of remembered the car parked outside the take-away food place but they didn't notice the driver. They thought it was about a week ago. A couple of truck drivers had seen her on the road too. One had reported her 'taking her life in her hands by zipping in and out between trucks in that little toy car. Obviously a city girl.'

Jack passed on the info to Cloncurry. Meanwhile Nina scoured every section of road between Prairie and Hughendon. Nothing.

The next day, Wednesday, had promised to be a stinker of a day, so Dr Sidowski decided to take his early morning run even earlier.

It was barely daylight when he set off. At the end of the street he had two options. Turn left and head onto the highway which would take you on to Mt Isa in one direction and Townsville in the other. Or turn right to the dead end of town where the roads lost more and more of their bitumen until they were just dirt tracks. Today he turned right and headed out across a flat plain, devoid of anything except the remains of a few long abandoned mining shacks and some scrubby bushland.

As the bitumen gave way to dirt, he was surprised to see a white Kia Hatchback parked at the front of the remnants of one of the shacks. He slowed down a little to see what was going on.

Daylight hadn't yet made its way into the shack but he thought he could see one?, two?, who knows how many shadows of people moving around inside. It was not the kind of car you saw much of around here and he assumed it was tourists. Bit early to be up and about, but who knows - maybe they had spent the night there. He kept running for another kilometer or so, following the track as it arced around a little to the right and over a bit of hill. At the top, he would turn around and head home.

This time there was something new on the horizon. A flash, a flame, he was too far away to see exactly but he was certain it was near to where he'd seen the car. He called the police station and the new constable answered the phone. Turley. That was his name. Turley Gardener. He said he'd get right onto it and he did. By the time Adam Sidowski had run back to the car, Turley Gardener had arrived. He was trying in vain to put out the fire with an emergency extinguisher. Within seconds it was obvious the car was about to explode. They took shelter behind the police car.

Next to arrive was the local fire truck, followed by Jack Harding. At this point, there was nothing they could do except wait until it was safe enough to get close to the car. The firefighters were already having a careful look through it to make certain the fire had been completely extinguished. The good news was that there was no body inside. The rest would be up to the forensics team to sort out.

Once they'd established that no one was in the car, they began looking for its driver. Probably the missing Amy Moreno. Dr Sidowski had mentioned that he thought he had seen someone - maybe more than one person inside the house, so while the new constable Turley got busy setting up yellow crime scene tape around the burnt out vehicle, Jack Harding and the doctor gingerly entered the shack.

They smelled her before they saw her. Not even the smell of burning rubber and petrol could disguise it. This time, the body was placed on her back, arms carefully by her side, the right side of her head so badly caved in that it had totally distorted the other side of her face. The beginnings of decomposition were also apparent. Dr Sidowski was just about to move towards the body when Jack stopped him.

"Adam, you can't be involved in this one mate, you're a witness, go home. We'll talk later.'

Doctor Lui arrived promptly from Hughenden's other medical practice to carry out the initial examination. He'd already contacted Professor Castleton to see if he would help and the Professor agreed it would be a good idea, as it sounded like it might be the same killer. He was already on his way and had arranged for the body to be collected and taken to the hospital in Cloncurry. A van arrived from the local funeral home and the body was carefully placed into a body bag and loaded up as per Professor Castleton's instructions. Once all the paperwork was complete and it left for the airport, Dr Lui walked out to his car and threw up. He'd done well to hold it together until then.

"A horrifying but fascinating situation," Professor Castleton had called it. 'Perhaps this victim could shed some light on the killer of the last one.'

The most obvious difference between the two deaths was that Amy Moreno had been dead considerably longer than Adele Farmer when the bodies were discovered. Amy had been deceased for at least 72 hours according to Dr Lui's assessment. The tissue deterioration was inconsistent, suggesting part of her body had been in contact with a cooler area. Once again the cause of death was obvious and suggested the same weapon - or at least the same type of weapon, as was used on Adele. And although the forensic team were still combing the shack for evidence, Professor Castleton was certain she'd been killed elsewhere because there was not a drop of blood or tissue anywhere in the shack, except on the couch where she'd been placed. And even that was minimal. He also suggested she had probably been wrapped in something - plastic, a metal or wooden box, something that left no fibers behind.

Professor Castleton's report also noted that Amy was estimated to have died between 72 and 80 hours previously - agreeing with Dr Lui. She had undergone breast augmentation surgery some years before and liposuction on her abdomen and buttocks more recently and showed some lung damage consistent with having been a smoker or working in a smoke-filled environment. There was nothing to indicate the cause of death was anything other than considerable blunt force trauma to the head. No defensive wounds or signs of violence to any other part of her body were noted. And no recent sexual activity was detected. Tissue and blood samples, plus a substance found under the fingernails of her right hand had been sent off for analysis and the Professor had carried out a quick blood type test. O positive again. 'Not really necessary because we know who she is, but I like to be consistent,' he had noted.

The burnt out car also gave up nothing to help identify the killer. Although there was one question both the forensics team and the police wanted an answer to. Where were her belongings? If she was moving from Brisbane to Cloncurry, surely she would have at least one suitcase of clothing with her? But there was no sign of anything like that in the car.

Meanwhile, Nina Forde was pretty pissed off that she'd been off duty when the murder had been called in. She wanted to see the body where it was found. To get a feel for what had happened there. Jack Harding had no problem with letting her onto the site, but he wouldn't allow her to see the body, she'd have to make do with photos. To keep her occupied, he made her the liaison officer for the family. She had the right temperament for it and he didn't feel he had the guts to face the grieving parents on a daily basis - especially when he had no answers.

Amy had been the youngest of four kids - all girls - and the dad and mum were getting on a bit. There was some question over who would identify the body. It would be left to her elderly father. He'd spent most of his working life driving trains so he'd seen a few horrific deaths over the years, but this was his own kid. His baby.

Both parents had been flown up in a police helicopter and the rest of the family would follow by road, so Nina's support would be important while they coped on their own.The scene of the crime - or at least where the body was found, was still roped off, but Nina drove the parents out as close to the shack as they could get and they left some flowers. Then they walked around a bit looking for who knows what and wondered why her? Why this? The same questions everyone has about a senseless death.

When they were ready to leave, Nina drove them back to town so that Jack Harding could address them in his formal capacity as a Senior Sergeant, that 'it's early days yet' and 'of course we'll keep you informed. Any questions, just contact Senior Constable Forde. She's your liaison officer. You have her card.'

What do you do in a situation like that? They went back to their motel and Amy's dad tried to forget the small part of Amy's face that Professor Castleton had patched up enough for an identification. The next day the other sisters arrived and Nina went through the process all over again. Then the family drove home together, none the wiser about what had happened.

Nina Forde was more optimistic about finding a link to the killer than Jack Harding. They had a car that still might give up something. They had some footprints from inside the shack - and - they had a witness. Dr Sidowski had actually seen the killer. He just had no idea what he looked like. But now there was a timeline. We knew when she'd been killed. And now we knew exactly when she'd been dumped. We just had to fill in the middle bits of where she'd been for the past 5 days since she was last sighted by the truckie. She was going to need more charts.

After Amy was found, Dr Sidowski had been given a lift home by the fire truck. He canceled all his morning appointments, gave his wife a heavily redacted version of events, showered and slept for a couple of hours. About mid afternoon, he was woken up by Jack Harding who suggested now might be a good time to talk while events were still fresh in his mind.

Once he started recounting the events of the morning, both men realized he'd seen quite a lot - but at the same time, not much at all - and certainly nothing that could identify the killer. He was certain the passenger side door of the car was open when he ran past, but it was closed when it went up in flames. He was also pretty certain he had seen the outlines of two people inside - but one of them could have been the victim. And he was absolutely certain there was no conversation.

"At that time of morning, there's nothing to hear except the sound of birds. Even if they were speaking softly I think I would have heard a murmur.'

There was also something else. Something unexpected at the side of the shack and then not there when they found the body. He hadn't paid any attention to it at the time, but there was a glint where the sun hit it. What was it? A wheelbarrow? A bin? He couldn't quite visualize it. But they both had the same big question. If the killer was there when Dr Sidowski ran by, how did he get away? There was no second car - he was certain of that - and if he had run back into town, he would have been seen by Constable Gardener surely.

Senior Constable Forde had already asked herself the same question and she thought she knew the answer. Lots of old mining shafts around there. You could hole up in one of those for a while, then get away. She'd already tracked down a map and was on her way with one of the Julia Creek Police constables who used to live around here.

Day one revealed nothing - but there were a lot of tyre tracks - mostly off-road bikes. She thought it might be worth getting forensics over to take a couple of casts. She also decided to set up a night watch to see if anything happened, or anyone appeared once it was dark and everyone had left the scene. Apart from being reminded how cold it could get out here at night, it revealed nothing. If the killer had been holed up there at all, he was now long gone.

Dr Lui had an even better suggestion. "He's like a magician - you know how they use distraction so you don't see the trick. For example, firstly there's the burning car. Everyone was paying attention just to that. Not looking at the shack at all. Then there's the distraction of the shack. We were only looking at the one with the body in it, but there's two more close by. He could easily have been hiding in one of those, and then with everyone coming and going he could just leave. Maybe he is someone who looked like he belonged there. There were lots of police from other places, firefighters, vans, trucks, locals milling around - he could have just blended right in. Even me - I pride myself on being observant, but I was feeling too sick to pay attention to anyone, I was just dealing with the body. You see, no one was looking for the killer.'

Jack Harding knew he was right about that. No one was looking for the killer. Not Constable Gardener and not Dr

Sidowski. They were all distracted by the burning car and the body.

The car gave up a couple of clues that might be important. For a start, the back seats had been placed in the horizontal position - maybe to carry a body. And the driver's seat had been moved further back than a person of Amy's height would sit. There was also a lot of polycyclic organic matter and slag present which suggested a lot of plastic had been there. Could have been garbage bags or just sheets of plastic. But a lot of it. Dr Lui had commented on the smell at the time and suggested that everyone at the site should have been wearing a mask, not just the fire crew. It was probably what Amy had been wrapped in.

Jack Harding went to the storage room and pulled out the whiteboard he had set up for the investigation into Adele Farmer's death. Underneath the information about Adele he started to add Amy's story. Nina Forde added her own notes on the same board, but in red. Most were just thoughts rather than facts although she'd done a lot of work on timings. How far could the killer travel from the place of death to the time of discovery of the bodies. Not that far for Amy because the killer would appear to have been on foot, but a long way for Adele because he had a car. As part of the initial investigation into Adele's death, they'd drawn a circle around the discovery site to the maximum distance he could have traveled. There were too many possibilities for it to be much use, but Nina was now suggesting they overlap a map showing how far the killer could get away from the Amy site, between the initial car fire and the police arriving. She'd worked out the distance on foot, or in a car that had been hidden unseen somewhere. It was a pretty crude estimation and without more information, it was hard to know if it would be useful or not, but it did suggest someone who knew the area pretty well, who was confident about getting away - or who had an accomplice.

They both stared at the board for a while, then wheeled it back into the cupboard. It hadn't told them anything.

A few days later Professor Castleton advised them that Amy's blood tests showed nothing out of the ordinary and that the substance under her fingernails was microfiber. The type used on steering wheel covers. He had requested a sample from Kia of their steering wheel covers to see if it was a match and it was.

"I'd say she gripped that steering wheel pretty hard at some stage.'

The Professor also agreed that the two deaths were related, judging by the injuries inflicted. He'd gone over all the information they'd gathered from Adele and checked it against everything they knew about Amy.

'Unfortunately there's no prints, no fibers, no unknown DNA present on either woman. The killer has done a good job of covering his - or her - tracks. We shouldn't assume it's a man - there's a lot of pretty strong women around here. A woman might have had some trouble moving Adele, but Amy was fairly petite.'

Jack Harding sent his report down to headquarters in Brisbane with the hopeful caveat that 'we are following up some timeline leads' and went home.

About 10pm that night he got a call from Detective Inspector Jules Banyenan from Brisbane CIB. She sounded bright and curious. She wondered if Jack could send her a copy of everything he had on the murders. Not just his official stuff. She was trying to see if there might be a link to similar crimes in other parts of the country.

"You've got a big transient population up there. All those miners and seasonal workers. Could be someone - you know - moving around. There's been a couple of nasty cases in W.A and NSW - could be connected. But please, don't stop looking up there either.'

The next morning, Jack sent through everything, including all of Nina's notes and charts and added a simple message.

It's either someone we know very well, or someone we don't know at all. But he certainly knows us.

Jules wondered what the bloody hell he meant by that.

After a few months, Jules Banyenan got back to Jack with the bad news that none of the other murders appeared to be related to Adele's or Amy's. 'But look I'd like to help in any way I can, so please keep in touch. Let's see if we can catch this bastard.'

They both took some comfort in the fact that it had been well over a year since Amy's body was found, so maybe the killer had left the area. "Or maybe you got a bit close to him Jack, and he's decided it's too risky to kill again.'

For the past year or so, Constable Turley Gardener had been dining out on his first-at-the-scene story. When he was first posted to Hughenden, he had wondered how an ambitious bloke like himself would ever be able to prove he deserved a shot at promotion, but these murders were testing them all and he figured he had as much of a chance as anyone to make the big breakthrough, so he was keen to follow up every tip that came in. In the meantime, there was still a lot of mundane policing to be done. So when his Senior Sergeant asked him to check out the report of an abandoned car over near Manoora, it was just another routine task.

Some weekend prospectors had spotted it, half buried in an old mine. It was pretty rusted up, but they were really more concerned about it littering the environment than the possibility that it was involved in any crime. Its plates were missing, so no doubt it had been stolen. At least the police would get it moved.

The first question Jack Harding had asked was 'What make of car is it?'

'An old Subaru mate. Looks like it was a navy blue color.'

That was a disappointment - he had been hoping it might have been Adele's car - although this one sounded like it had been out in the open a bit long. Still it didn't warrant a trip by him. He would send out the junior constable.

Constable Gardener took a couple of photos and poked around inside the rusty interior. Who knows how long it had been there, but it definitely wasn't the missing hire car. Under the bonnet, someone had tried to scratch out the VIN number, but there was enough left for identification. He entered it in the stolen vehicles register and it came up as reported stolen from Rockhampton just over 4 years ago. He arranged for it to be towed to Manoora where Rockhampton police could decide what to do with it.

It was about 5 kilometers across country to get back to the sealed road that led back to Hughenden. You couldn't rush it because the place was littered with the remains of old mines and numerous rabbit warrens. Blowing out a tyre would be a pain in the arse, worse if you did an axle. Down the way a bit, he saw a huge piece of plastic flapping in the breeze. He thought he'd do the right thing and pick it up. He stopped and walked over to the plastic.

'Fuckin' hell" Poking through the sand was a skull, badly damaged, weathered, but recognizable. He bent down to take a closer look. There was also what looked like ribs just visible.

It took him a couple of minutes to steady his hand enough to call it in. Then he sat and waited for the investigation team to arrive.

No need for a doctor this time, just a forensics team and that would take time to get out here, but Jack Harding and Nina Forde arrived pretty quickly. They were both staring at the skull. The right side had been violently crushed by something, just like the others.

While they waited, Jack called Jules Banyenan. "I think we've got another one."

4

Jules wanted to move the remains to Brisbane where there was more expertise rather than to Mt Isa. Jack thought that was a good idea too - if only to spread responsibility for solving the crime a little wider.

He'd barely hung up when Professor Castleton was on the phone. He was a bit miffed when he found out about the Brisbane move. He didn't say so, but it was pretty obvious he thought that putting the best people on the case would include him. He told Jack that he didn't want to go to Brisbane anyway - didn't like the place much - and had more important work to do around here - so he was happy to make identifying the skeleton someone else's problem. "But keep me up to date with developments will you, I want to see this case solved as much as you do."

It took a whole day to release the skeleton from the ground. Even so, parts of it were missing. The team carefully packed the remains and sent them off to the forensic anthropologist in Brisbane. At the same time, they continued combing a larger area looking for the missing feet and arm and anything else that might offer a clue as to who she was. They had also gathered up bits of rag that had probably been the victims clothes - a rusted zip and metal studs and remains of a synthetic shirt that had resisted destruction. The large sheet of plastic that had once wrapped the body was the kind of standard stuff you could buy by the metre at any big hardware store. It was badly torn in places - probably by wild dogs and was heavily discoloured underneath the skeleton. After two days on the site, a few more bits of bone had been found and were sent off to Brisbane, but nothing else.

The major concern - especially for Constable Gardener, was that the skeleton looked small. It was horrifying to think it might be a child - but the team that dug up the body assured him it was a slightly built, adult woman.

Back in town, there was a palpable sense of fear. It didn't seem to matter that the skeleton had been possibly buried there years ago and unearthed by recent flooding and soil erosion. it felt as though it had only happened yesterday. Three female bodies in a small place like this, all with the same type of facial injury. Surely it was some nasty bastard with a grudge against the area using it as a dumping ground. It couldn't be one of us.

Back in Brisbane, the chief forensic anthropologist, a bloke named Mark Simpson, was quick to get back to Jules Banyenen with some initial information.

The skeleton belonged to a woman - estimated to be between 28 and 35 years old. She'd had a broken left arm - probably as a child, and several ribs showed signs of breaks and healing as an adult. Her right arm was missing below the elbow and both feet also - but there was no sign that they had been severed. More likely removed by wild dogs at some point. Her teeth and jaw had been knocked around so badly by the blunt force trauma that killed her, that a great deal of reconstruction would have to be carried out before dental records could be used for identification. Even then - it might prove useless. Considerable weathering of the bones suggested she'd been buried as long as 7 years ago but more likely 5, judging from the style of the remains of her clothes. He was hoping to extract some useful

DNA that might give us a better idea of who she was - but he was already pretty certain she was originally from South East Asia. He recommended the forensic team enlarge the search area for signs of the missing body parts.

The first step in identifying the latest victim was to check out all the missing persons reports going back as far as 7 years - just to be certain. There couldn't be that many women just 150cm tall, between 28 and 35 who'd gone missing in that time. In fact, after a number of weeks of searching and cross matching, it turned out there were none that hadn't since been accounted for. So they then sent out details to all the South East Asian embassies in case they had records of women reported missing in Australia. Surprisingly there were quite a large number. 53 in total, but almost all were from more recent times, under 25 and mostly taller than our victim. In some cases there was no record of these missing women even entering the country - despite the families insisting that they had. The consensus was that the majority were trafficked sex workers. In the end, it all came down to just 6 women. 3 had been missing 5 years or less and 1 had been missing for 10 years, but had reportedly been seen in New Zealand as recently as a year ago. That left two. Both from well to do families and in Australia on study visas. One from Thailand and the other from Cambodia.

Both families were asked to provide DNA samples from a parent or sibling. We'd just have to wait.

It was barely 8am and Jack Harding was just arriving at the station with his morning coffee. A young man, heavily bearded, tall and well built shoved a business card into his face. It was one of Jacks own, badly tattered and with a mobile number scrawled on the back.

"Excuse me, are you Senior Sergeant Harding?"

"That'd be me."

"I'm Jason Farmer - Adele's brother.'

Jack took a deep breath and looked down at his feet, then at Jason. "Come in."

As it turned out, Jason had been on assignment in Antarctica when Adele was killed and so he wasn't at her funeral or at the memorial held in Hughenden. Since being back, he'd relied on family for details - of which there weren't many. He was frustrated by the lack of progress and thought he'd come and see the site where she was found and see if the Senior Sergeant Jack Harding listed on the card had anything new to add. When Jack looked at the card he could see the number on the back was Senior Constable Forde's mobile number. He'd given that out to Adele's mother so that she could call any time but after the brief memorial service, no one ever did call.

'I wish I could give you some answers Jason, but it seems we just keep getting more and more questions. We suspect we have a serial killer. There's at least one other victim and possibly two. But out here there's a lot of open space - there's no video surveillance cameras on every corner. And despite extensive searching, we still haven't even found Adele's car. We just keep hoping the victims themselves can tell us something - or the killer makes a mistake. It could take years - or we could have a breakthrough tomorrow - but I promise you, people are working on it - both here and in Brisbane. She hasn't been forgotten.'

'This one' - he signaled over to Nina Forde, ' she's so determined to find out what happened, that she's always testing out some theory or other in her own time. I can get her to take you out to the site if you like. There's a garden place just down the street - just near the statue of the big dinosaur if you want to take some flowers.'

He called Nina over.

'Senior Constable Forde - this is Jason Farmer - Adele's brother, could you take him out to the place we found her?'

There wasn't a great variety of flowers available, but in the end, Jason settled on a bunch of mixed coloured orchids. He climbed into the car, the flowers sitting awkwardly on his lap.

"Do you get many dinosaurs around here then?'

"We're famous for it - this one is called Muttaburrasaurus - or Mutt by his friends.. There's a whole dinosaur trail that goes through Richmond, Winton and here....'

There was a pause, then....

"So do you think you'll get him?"

"I think we already know who he is - we just don't know that we know.'

"Excuse me??"

'It's someone who knows this area very well. Knows how to make a quick getaway. Where he can go to disappear. It's not someone passing through - not one of the fly-in, fly-out miners. This person knows every inch of the landscape around here. ....Doesn't mean he lives here though - but I'm certain he's known in the area, maybe even well known by us, which is why I think he's gone quiet. We might have been getting too close to him.'

Soon the buildings thinned out to nothing and they arrived at the spot.

"This is the place?'

'Yep'

'In the middle or on the side of the road?'

'Sort of here. - carefully laid out.'

'What about the guy who found her?'

'Yeah well we were lucky it was him - someone else might have roared along here and right over the top of her. It's pitch black around here at night.'

'And you still haven't found the car?'

'No - I think he burns them. He set fire to the other one.'

'It's a horrible trick of fate you know - her being killed by a blow to the head. She used to suffer really bad migraines and if one was really bad she'd say it was like being hit in the head by a brick.'

'We don't think it was a brick.'

'....still....well I guess that's it then.'

'Take as much time as you need.'

He placed the flowers to the side of the road, walked around a bit looking at nothing in particular and then they headed back to town in silence. Nina made a mental note to talk to Jack about the migraines. Maybe she had one at the time and stopped somewhere to sleep it off.

'Did she have any special medication for the migraines?'

'I don't know. Why do you ask?'

'Always looking for new clues.'

'Mum might know - I'll call her.'

Senior Constable Forde tried her best to tune out the conversation. It was personal and highly emotional.

He hung up and wrote a name down on the back of the receipt from the plant shop.

'She used to take Sumatriptan. It's an over the counter thing. You don't need a prescription.'

Now Nina knew she had to check the toxicology reports. She was almost excited.

Jason looked her in the eyes as he handed over the bit of paper.

'You think it was something to do with her having a migraine don't you?'

'It's possible... it's worth looking into.....Every new bit of information is worth checking. She might have stopped somewhere to buy some of that - what did you call it?'

'Sumatriptan.'

He was glad he'd come and seen things for himself. He felt reassured that these guys really were on the case - especially Senior Constable Forde. She might have suffered a bad migraine and stopped somewhere to sleep it off. He ran the scenario over and over in his head. It made sense.

Made sense to Jack Harding too. He put in a request to every pharmacy along her planned route to ask if they'd sold that particular medication on that day to anyone. No one had. As one of the pharmacists said, 'Regular sufferers tend to carry some with them if they're going to be away from home, but if her migraine was that bad, she probably went somewhere quiet and dark to sleep it off. Have you checked motels along the way?'

They had, but Jack thought it might be worth checking again. In the meantime, they'd put in a call to Dr Sidowski to ask if Sumatripton would have shown up in the blood tests.

'Probably not - it clears the body pretty quickly, so it's more likely to show up in a urine test than a blood test.'

'What about side effects that might show up in the blood?'

"Now you're above my pay grade. Professor Castleton would know the answer to that."

So they called the Professor.

'Well a fairly extreme side effect is what is called Serotonin Syndrome and if you are looking to confirm a diagnosis, there are a number of blood tests you can carry out which will give you an answer -but they are only usually carried out if the patient is quite ill. Are we talking about one of our girls here, because we didn't look for this in either case. Why would we? The medication certainly wouldn't show up in their blood..... By the way, any news on the remains that were sent to the experts in Brisbane?'

'We're waiting on some DNA results to try and identify her. We think she might be one of two women who were reported missing at that time.'

'Hmmm..interesting - then you don't think she's a local then?'

'No.'

'Oh well, hope I was able to help in some way.'

'Thanks Professor. Sorry to bother you.'

'Not at all - call anytime.'

So the blood tests would be a dead end - but not the scenario.

Once word got around about the migraine medication, a young girl who worked in the Post Office at Richmond remembered that one of the ladies from the Richmond Historical Society had come in complaining that 'there's a young woman out there throwing up.' The Post Office Assistant had gone out and asked her if she needed help 'but she said not to worry - that it was a migraine and that she was going to get out of the sun, take her medication and sleep it off.' She couldn't describe the woman beyond, youngish, big dark glasses, a sun hat and a towel over her mouth. And she was wearing a dress or skirt. Not trousers. The woman had walked away towards the hotel and she assumed that's where she went.

But nope - she hadn't gone to the hotel. Not at least according to the hotel registry. Not to any other place in town either. But it was a step forward. She had needed help and had to have found someplace or other to sleep it off. Jack Harding was certain she had accepted help from someone.......just the wrong someone unfortunately.

Jack and Nina wheeled their white board out from the cupboard and wrote up the new information. It looked as though whatever happened to Adele Farmer, started in Richmond - now the last place she had been seen alive. He sent this new information to Jules Banyenan and the police at Broken Hill who could stop looking for her missing car around there.

Jules Banyenan knew Jack was right. Richmond was probably the key for Adele Farmers death. But it was only a small town, everyone knew everyone. If you took out the women and kids and the elderly, there weren't that many likely suspects. More likely to be someone from the region who just happened to be in Richmond at that time. She went back through Jack's notes. There had been a lot of groundwork done in all the towns along the highway there. Door knocking, posters in shop windows, checking any security videos for suspicious activity. Every cafe and petrol stop worker on duty at the time had been questioned. There was nothing out of the ordinary. At the time, even a woman throwing up outside the Post Office didn't get a mention. It didn't seem important then. And after Adele had been identified, they'd traveled back over the route she would have taken and gone through the same procedure. Broken Hill police had also carried out a search not just along the main road, but down many of the dirt roads that led off the highway. A helicopter also searched the area looking for signs of an abandoned car, but of course now we knew she'd gone a long way past Broken Hill.

Jules decided to fly up to Hughenden and go through both cases with Jack Harding. Maybe tracing Adele's last movements around Richmond might reveal something. Adele Farmer had no reason to be there if she was heading to Mt Isa, Richmond was quite a way out of the way, so they'd need to look for a connection. It was always possible that Jack suspected something - or someone - that he didn't want to put in writing. Maybe that feisty smart-arsey Senior Constable - what was her name - Forde, yeah Forde…maybe she'd turned up something. She'd already turned up the migraine theory and been right about that.

Jack and Nina Forde were both glad to see her. They dragged out their whiteboard with all the known information about Adele and Amy, but just a big ? for the as yet unidentified skeleton. Jules underlined the question mark on the whiteboard.

'She looks like she belongs here because of the damage to her skull, but we can't be certain until she's identified. And it worries me that there's such a big gap between the mystery woman's murder and these two. 5, 6, - possibly 7 years. What happened during this time? And why suddenly two more so close together? And now nothing again for what? - a year and a half? If she's a victim we have to be looking for a killer who has been around here for 6 or 7 years at least. What are we saying? He kills someone, goes quiet for 5 or 6 years and then kills 2 women in a little over a year?'

Nina Forde piped in.

"Or…he was out of the area for a couple of years..or possibly in prison..or just didn't have the opportunity. He could have had housing issues, or money problems, or health issues - something that kept him occupied. I've already put in a request for a list of violent offenders who were jailed up to 7 years ago and released in the past 2 years. We might find someone there.'

Richmond might be a small town, but it was big on space. It would only take a few minutes for someone to get out of town and into nothingness, where anything could happen. Just one street back from the pub she was seen walking towards, you were almost out of town. There would have been few people on the street - and no witnesses at all if she'd gone down one of the lanes. She could have headed to her car to sleep off the migraine and someone attacked her, dumped her body and drove away. Just like that. It would explain the lack of defensive wounds. And it tied in with the Amy killing too. Maybe Amy was also asleep in her car when the killer attacked. And Adele's hire car wouldn't have attracted attention either. Every second car around the Richmond area was some kind of SUV.

Jack rubbed the frustration from his eyes.

'Well she hadn't been raped, but she may have been robbed. We never found her bag or phone and she wasn't wearing any jewelry or a watch. And we've never found the car. Just as we never found the belongings of Amy Moreno. The only difference is the car. Maybe in Adeles' case the killer needed the car to get away.'

Nina pursed her lips. 'Then why did he drive all the way here? There are lots of places around Richmond where he could have dumped her. And why drive here with Amy…. It must be something to do with being familiar with the area. As for the car - well personally, I think he burns the cars. Maybe we can't find Adele's car because it's burnt out somewhere. I mean how would you know where to look first? We've searched the area around where we found her and now that we know about Richmond, we've been back there. Nothing. The car could be sitting in an old mine shaft for all we know.'

'Or….."Jules tapped the whiteboard, "Or he had to burn Amy's car because it had too much incriminating evidence in it and that Doctor…what's his name? Sidowski…he ruined his plans by turning up so early in the morning before he'd had a chance to clean up. He might have been planning to get rid of this car the same way he got rid of Adeles'. By just driving away in it.'

Nina butted in. 'But we don't know how he got rid of Adele's car. And anyway, if he uses the cars to get away - how did he get away from the shack where Amy was found?'

It was the same question everyone - even the inexperienced Constable Gardener had asked themselves time and time again. They'd even gone as far as recreating the scene, placing everyone where they remember being on the day, to see if they could spot any possible answers. Dr Lui's explanation was the best so far. They'd all been so distracted by what was going on with the car and the body, that they didn't see anything else. The one thing they all agreed on, was yes -he had obviously torched Amy's car to get rid of evidence - but surely he wouldn't have done that if he didn't have a plan B to escape. After all, the Doctor had kept running, giving him plenty of time to drive away and word was only just getting out linking the car to Amy. She might not have been found for another day or two, giving the killer plenty of time to do whatever he wanted with the car.

Just as they were about to head off to Richmond to retrace Adele's movements, Jules received an email that stated the DNA belonging to the skeletal remains did not match the missing Thai national. They were still waiting on Cambodia which would take a lot longer. Both parents had died since the missing persons report had been filed, and it had taken time to track down her siblings, two of whom were conveniently living in Canada. They were hopeful a sample would be tested sometime this week.

As they were leaving, Jack pointed to the poster that had just been put up in the reception area of the station. **$100,000 REWARD for information.** Below the headline was a photo of Adele and Amy and a blank square filled with a question mark to signify the mystery woman. The reward was being offered by the local business association. They were concerned the deaths were having a deleterious effect on the area's reputation. There were big projects at stake and Hughenden had worked hard to overcome its wild west reputation to become a family friendly town. These murders were undoing all that good work.

"They're putting them up all over the region. Right up to Mt Isa, down to Broken Hill, right out to Townsville and Innisfail on the coast.'

Jules noticed that underneath the general request to contact your local police station, they had also listed her number as 'or call direct'. She was a bit pissed off about that. No one had asked her permission and the last thing she needed was a whole heap of red herrings. Better for the local police to check tips out first and weed out the rubbish. She asked Jack to insist her number was removed on the next batch that went out.

Richmond is a small, tidy town - most famous as the "Fossil Capital." The whole region relied heavily on family tourism and if Hughenden was seen as a dangerous place for women to drive though - well - Richmond would be too. So they were right behind the push by the Hughenden business community to offer a reward. They'd even contributed to it. So on the one hand, they welcomed the arrival of Jules Banyenan and Jack Harding and on the other hand, they wanted to keep their presence as low-key as possible, so as not to spook the visitors.

The local Senior Constable joined them as they started their walk at the Post Office. He pointed out that Adele had headed off down Goldring Street towards the pub. The Post Office assistant - Verity - hadn't stayed around out front to see where the woman actually went. Instead she'd gone inside to get a bucket of water to wash away the vomit. When she'd come back out, there was no sign of the woman. This had all happened mid afternoon, about 2.30pm. Jules noticed that many of the buildings on that side of the road had side lanes that ran through to the street behind. Adele could easily have taken a shortcut up one of those.

The local police had gone through footage from the few security cameras in the area. The police station of course, the court house around the corner, Kronosaurus Korner and Museum and one of the petrol stations. The car had made an appearance at Kronosaurus Korner at 4.27pm but was just passing through and you couldn't see who was driving it. It was at least something. 4.27pm was only a couple of hours earlier than the time of death, but considering the distance to Hughenden, it must have been headed there then. Unfortunately due to the car having tinted windows, they had no hope of identifying the driver. They'd already checked any security cameras in Hughenden around that time and seen no sign of the car there, so either it was disposed of after leaving Richmond or the killer was smart enough to avoid the main streets.

As they drove back to Hughenden, Jules formulated the most likely scenario. "So it looks like she was probably out of it, asleep in her car, someplace in the shade and he's tried to rob her. She wakes up and he hits her across the head with something before she can scream. Or maybe he hits her while she's still asleep. Then he drives out here - away from Richmond and dumps her on the road. Pulls down her pants to make it look like sexual assault, then hopes someone will come speeding along and flatten her making it even harder to identify her. He then drives her car away. Somewhere far enough from Hughenden and Richmond not to be found, but close enough to somewhere he can get back to on foot - or where he has another car waiting.'

Jack Harding thought she was probably right, 'But it's a risky scenario. It was still broad daylight when the killer drove her to Hughenden. If he was a local - tinted windows or no - he could have been seen and recognised.' He paused for a minute. 'I mean we keep saying 'he' but Professor Castleton keeps reminding us that the killer could be a woman, that does change things..'

Back at the station, they added the latest details to the white board. Jules stared at it for a long time, made some notes and went to her motel room to catch up on emails and phone calls. The next day she flew back to Brisbane.

As promised, a week later the results of DNA tests taken by the relatives of the missing Cambodian woman arrived from Canada. They were not a match.

Meanwhile, the posters offering the $100,000 reward were generating regular tips. Some were from kids causing trouble, some were from 'cookers' who had a range of outlandish conspiracy theories, some were from psychics who believed they had received messages from the other side and a few were well-meaning, possible tips. None of them led anywhere except down the rabbit hole. The case was cooling rapidly.

5

A couple of months after the first posters went up, Jules Banyenan received a call from Adelaide CIB. A woman named Cheryl Hinkler had come in claiming she knew who the skeleton belonged to.

Cheryl had been a sex worker at Manoora until about 5 years ago and a woman she worked with named Lily Fernandez had gone missing about a year before she left the town.

According to Cheryl, the missing woman was from somewhere in the Philippines which sat comfortably with the South East Asian scenario - and she claimed to still have a box of personal stuff that belonged to the Fernandez woman. She'd hung onto it all these years in case she ran into Lily somewhere.

'She says there's nothing valuable in the box but there's some personal stuff that could help. Letters and photos. Hard to know if she's credible or not - there have been a number of substance abuse problems and petty crime convictions along the way, but we taped the interview. I'll send it through. She's very keen to get the money. She certainly looks like she could use it.'

Jules grabbed a coffee, opened the file and pressed play. On one side of a desk sat the interviewing detective, facing away from the camera. On the other side was Cheryl. She looked about 50 though she was probably younger. Jules could see she'd done her best to look presentable. An ironed shirt, hair neatly combed. A bit of makeup but not over the top. But she had that worn-weary look of someone who has been through too much and not come out very well. After the usual chit chat about the date and time and who was in the room, Cheryl told her story with as much confidence as she could muster.

"About 8 or 9 years ago I had to get out of Adelaide. I owed a lot of money to the wrong people.... and they were getting nasty. Anyway I ended up in Manoora. It's a little mining place up Mt Isa way. Not great, but it was the last place the debt collectors would come looking. I was doing a bit of sex work up there. '

She squirmed in her chair. " - I looked better than this in those days. I've had some health issues. - Anyway most of the girls came and went pretty quick -but I made friends with Lily. Lily Fernandez her name was. She'd been there a while - well a few months. I think she fancied one of her regulars. (She rolls her eyes) Big mistake.

Things were pretty normal until about a week before she disappeared. She started acting a bit sort of funny. I dunno - nervous, maybe upset about something. Whatever was bothering her, she wouldn't talk to me about it. I didn't push it. We all had our secrets. Anyway one morning she just gets up and goes off without a word to anyone. Must have been pretty early because no one saw her go. I don't know how she left either - she didn't have a car or anything, but there you go.

Of course back then, at the time, none of us really thought she'd disappeared. We just thought she was with a client. Struck it lucky with someone willing to pay her to stick around for a day or so. ....Yeah it does happen sometimes. But she didn't call - and then when we tried to call her, it went to voicemail. Then ...(mumbled something unintelligible).

So after a few days I rang the police in.... Winton....yeah Winton and spoke to some kid there. He asked me to come in and make a formal report. I couldn't get there for a few days and when I did make it, I don't think he took me seriously. He wrote stuff down, I signed something. That's it. Never heard from him again. I rang a couple of times but they just kept telling me they had no news.

But what bothered me was that she left this. (She pushes a battered enameled box across the table.) Open it. (The detective opens it) You see it's filled with all her precious things. Photos, her rosary beads, some letters from home - she came from the Philippines you know. Well I thought, this is stuff she wouldn't leave behind. She left all her clothes too. I didn't keep those. Too small for any of us. (She pulls the box back to her) So I've kept this stuff for years in case she ever came back. But I think this body you found - this skeleton - I reckon it's her.'

There was a bit more chit-chat about where she lives (with an older sister) and how she's got a proper job now and how she heard about the reward. (From one of the girls who works in the brothel where Cheryl now works as a cleaner) She reluctantly agrees to leave the box of memories behind after she is given a receipt with the detective's business card stapled to it, and leaves. The detective then notes that he will forward on a copy of this interview and the box belonging to Lily Fernandez to Detective Inspector Jules Banyenan at Brisbane CIB and the interview ends.

Jules puts in a request for information about Lily Fernandez from Australian Immigration and the Winton Police. There are entirely different officers at Winton now and so they will have to go back through the files.

Immigration was much quicker. Lily Fernandez had come to Australia on a student visa to study nursing, but she had overstayed her visa and there was no evidence she had ever actually engaged in any type of nursing course. Letters advising her that she faced deportation had been sent to her last known address in Sydney 8 years ago - and she had been in contact with immigration officials after the first letter, asking what she had to do to sort it out. Nothing since. Bureaucracy being what it is, there were various attempts to find her and she was on the watch list at every international airport in Australia, but she had never turned up. It was assumed that like many other overstayers, she'd adopted a new name and 'disappeared' into a new life somewhere where she wouldn't attract attention.

The next day Winton police came back with the news that they had found the report, but it appeared that it was never acted upon. Winton Police had no idea where the people who worked there at the time were stationed now - or even if they were still on the force. "Do you want us to track them down?' Jules thought it was too late to worry about that now.

Once Lily's precious box arrived, Jules arranged for a translator to look at the letters. There were two which seemed to be from her mother. One in which she thanked Lily for the money she had sent and another with news of the death of her grandmother. Both had the same address in Cebu City on the back. There was a photo of a very happy young woman clowning about with an older man, (Cheryl had said this was Lily but she didn't know who the bloke was) and a couple of faded family photos that looked like they'd been taken in the 80's. Plus some rosary beads that were made from different coloured polished stones, a child-sized crucifix and a birthday card written in English with a gushing message and lots of kisses, signed by Manny. ('I think he was her ex-soul mate.' Cheryl had said about this)

Jules phoned the Philippines Embassy and put in a request to supply any information they could about Lily Fernandez.

She emailed the photo of Lily minus the older man and gave them details of the last known family address in Cebu City, plus the name of her dead grandmother. The embassy had no record of the Fernandez family making any request for information about her. Lily had certainly never been reported as missing, but they would look into it.

Just over four weeks later the Embassy was pleased to advise that they had tracked down Lily's father. Her mother had unfortunately died of COVID and her father had gone to live with a family member in Quezon City. They passed on the contact details of a senior detective there for Jules to deal with directly.

The Detective was helpful but insisted that the police would first need to find out if the Fernandez family knew where Lily was, or if they had any recent contact with her before they hinted that she might be deceased. If they were then satisfied that she was missing - presumed deceased - they would go through the official processes necessary to take DNA. But it would all take time.

'We don't have the ready access to the pathology services you have in Australia. There's always a waiting list. I'll have to call in some favours in Manila.'

But he assured Jules Banyenan that he would do all he could to help resolve this matter and offered his total co-operation - although he couldn't promise the family would be willing to provide DNA.

A few months passed and Jules received news that relatives of Lily Fernandez had been found and that the request for DNA would move forward. Everyone involved in the case was still excited by the prospect of at last identifying the unidentified skeleton, so another victim was the last thing anyone was expecting. But there she was, in a crime scene photo sent through by Jack Harding with the simple message. We've got another one.

Jules called him back. He sounded defeated.

"There's a bit of a difference. This one is in her car and we know who she is. She manages a mini market in Cloncurry - and she's only recently deceased - less than an hour before she was found apparently. We also have a clear understanding of her last movement during the day - including a few witnesses who saw her at various places. We might get lucky this time.'

'Where is she now?'

'She's been moved to the morgue in Mt Isa.'

'I don't want anyone who has had anything to do with the last two bodies to touch her - do you understand? I'm coming up there straight away and I'm bringing people with me. Oh and don't let anyone touch the car either.'

Jack was taken aback by her reaction and tone of voice. "Ok, Ok, will do.'

Professor Castleton was already at the morgue and fully gowned up and ready to go to work when Jack told him to stop. The professor found it all 'highly unprofessional and a bit insulting given my credentials, 'but alright, if that's what they want.'

The local forensic team had also started taking fingerprints and blood samples and photographing blood splatter and tyre prints. But the car was still where it had been found - down a rather steep embankment where it wasn't immediately visible from the road. There'd been some heavy rain though the area the day before and the ground was boggy in parts, leaving distinct tyre treads that indicated it had gone off the road without any attempt at braking. And of course they were dealing with the dark. Even the portable spotlights they had rigged up at the scene were no substitute for daylight.

Sarah was only found so quickly because her husband had expected her home and she wasn't answering her phone. He was concerned she'd had an accident somewhere. The police assured him there had been no accident reports that afternoon but they would take a run out of town to see if the car broken down somewhere. After 30 kilometers or so, they had found nothing but a couple of old tyres abandoned on the roadside. The only petrol station in the area was on the other side of the road about 10 kilometers back. They'd checked in there anyway, but their security cameras only focussed on their own side of the road, so there was nothing. They went on another 10 k's or so, then, just as they were about to do a U-turn and head back to town, a sharp-eyed constable spotted what looked like a car, behind some scrub. It was off the road a bit, but definitely worth investigating.

At first they thought she'd run off the road, but the car wasn't damaged at all. As for the woman inside - well that was a different story.

The attack on her hadn't happened long ago because she was still warm. They called it in. The drivers license in her wallet said her name was Sarah Newhouse. She was 47 and lived at an address in Cloncurry.

The police helicopter landed with Inspector Jules Banyenan, a senior forensic pathologist, a forensic scientist and a forensic assistant. Jules and the pathologist went straight to the morgue. Ray Newhouse sat gray-faced in the waiting room with his two sons, 20 year old Nick and 17 year old Jess. They were both red-faced from crying and frustrated by not being able to see their mum. Jules Banyenan had the tough job of having to explain that 'due to the nature of her injuries facial recognition might not be possible. Ray wanted to see her anyway.

'We need to examine her first for clues while the crime scene is still fresh.' The words sounded horrible, but that was the truth of it.

Sarah had been hit several times around the face and head by a heavy blunt object which was quickly identified as a cricket bat. One of the boys had obviously left his bag of gear in the back of the car, and the murderer had made use of it. But once again there was a problem. There were no defensive wounds. Why would she sit there while the killer hunted around for a weapon and then attacked her. Her bag had been rifled through too, but nothing appeared to be taken. Phone, wallet, all there. The only recent calls she'd made were to her husband. The last time she called was 2.30pm and she'd hung up after a few seconds. A few minutes later he'd called back, but she hadn't picked up. Nor had she answered any of the other 15 calls and 7 text messages he'd made to her throughout the afternoon.

Apart from the damage to her face and head, there was little sign of violence, but drag marks and blood to the side of the car suggested she had been outside of the vehicle when the attack took place, then placed back into the car. A crude attempt had been made to cover the blood on the ground without much success. There was just too much of it.

At the back of the car, there were a lot of scuffed footprints and sharp drag marks. A short distance away, they stopped abruptly. A little further away still, there was a broken trail of what looked like motorcycle tracks. These didn't lead either to - or from the car, or the main road - they just disappeared into the scrub. And because of the previous rain, water had soaked up into the indents, making it hard to tell how long they'd been there. There were also indentations that looked like footprints, but with no sole pattern. Largish - so likely a man's - but they didn't appear to lead to or from the car either.

It was mysterious enough to rope off for further investigation in the morning. It strongly suggested more than one person was involved.

It was still too soon to get a clear picture of bruising but there were no obvious signs of strangulation. The pathologist took blood and tissue samples and emptied the contents of her stomach. It appeared as though she hadn't eaten for several hours but the stomach contents had a strange acidic odor. 'Maybe she was poisoned or drugged first. Could explain the lack of defense wounds - but drugging *and* bashing? Bit of an overkill.'

The rest of the autopsy revealed nothing additional that could have contributed to her death. There were some fatty deposits around her liver and a hernia at the entrance to her stomach - but apart from that she appeared in good health. There was a fresh small crack in a rib on the left side of her body, but this was probably caused by her seatbelt when she was dragged from the car rather than the assault.

As the body settled, signs of bruising began appearing on the upper inside parts of both arms indicating she had been pulled - probably from the car and then pushed back into it. The bruises were wide and misshapen, as if the killer was wearing large gloves - like working gloves. Until the results of the stomach contents were known, we would not know if they played any part in her death.

In cases like these, the prime suspect is always the husband, but in this case Ray and his sons all had perfect alibis. Ray was a mechanic and he was at work all day around an hour and a half away in Cloncurry - and in full view of numerous customers and passers by. Jess, the younger boy was at school all day and Nick had gone to Julia Creek to have a game of tennis with his mates before heading back to Uni. Jules Banyenan was relieved that they were all clearly out of the picture. Domestic violence was a nasty business.

There were a number of sightings of either Sarah or her car that day. She was caught on camera at 11.02 am entering and 11.07am leaving her bank. (Records would show she withdrew $500 from the ATM}

A local traffic warden had moved her along from parking illegally in front of the building that housed Professor Castletons Pathology Laboratories at 11.30am.

There was footage of her at a nearby pharmacy at 12.15pm and then entering the foyer Professor Castleton's office at 12.27pm. She left looking happy enough at 12.40pm. But then as photos of her car were circulated, one of the other tenants in the building recalled seeing her car parked out the back when he left for home at about 3.30pm. He noticed it because usually the only car that was ever parked there was the professor's off road truck - but it wasn't there now - just this silver gray Toyota Land Cruiser that he'd never seen before. He hadn't noticed anyone sitting in the car.

There were enough links to make Professor Castleton a possible suspect. But the guy was an academic, over 60 and highly unlikely to bash anyone's head in. Still, he had questions to answer.

He was happy to talk to Jules - flattered almost that he had something to contribute to the case. They all agreed that in retrospect it was just as well he hadn't done the autopsy as he went through details of how he'd spent his day.

'Yes, well I know Sarah from the supermarket in Cloncurry - but not that well. Last time I was down there she came up to me in the street and complained that she was having quite severe menopausal symptoms. Dreadful hot flushes and mood swings- trouble sleeping - but the local GP wouldn't prescribe hormone replacement therapy for her. I believe she said it was because she had a history of blood clots and her mother and older sister had both died from ovarian cancer. ... Well that's reason enough really......Anyway she knew that I have an international reputation for my work in developing natural alternatives to synthetic medicines and she asked if I could recommend something that might help. Hormonal therapies are not something I have been working on, although there are a number of promising plants that have been identified.... '

He took a deep breath and thought for a minute.

'..But anyway I suggested to her that next time she was in Mt Isa, if she bought a couple of the over the counter menopause treatment products from the pharmacy or health food store, I would take a look at the list of ingredients and suggest which one might be the most effective. Which is what she did...... that's why she was at my office that morning. She hadn't made an appointment or anything, just turned up with something that contained Magnolia bark, black Cohosh and something else. Made in a reputable laboratory. I had no idea if they would work - although I believe they have been used for centuries in folk medicine....I told her they certainly wouldn't do her any harm. Then she left. I think she was in a hurry to get home before her son got home from school.'

'So why was her car parked at the back of your building?'

'What do you mean?' The only vehicle which is ever parked at the back is my truck.'

'Her car was seen there about 3pm'

'Aah well I wouldn't have seen it then. I left around 1 o'clock to check out some *Citrus Glauca* that Aunty Lydia reckoned she'd come across about 20 kilometers out of town. Don't normally find them growing wild around here so I wanted to see

them for myself .....- They have quite a number of health bene-
fits you know... Anyway, her car wasn't there then. Only mine. '

The Professor appeared to drift away for a bit, as though he
had nothing more to say - then he continued.

'I picked Aunty up at her place - as arranged - and we went
searching for the lime trees. I took some photos......here have
a look......(he swiveled his laptop around towards Jules and
clicked on some photos) We picked some limes, I collected
some leaves, then I drove Aunty back to her place and we had
a cuppa. - After that I came back here...parked out the front
while I dropped this off (waves his camera) - entered the location of the lime bushes into my computer - and downloaded
the photos, then locked up my office and drove home. Heather
and Isaac, my lab assistants, were still here working when I left
at about 4.30-ish - check with them. I didn't go around the back
at all, so I have no idea if her car was there or not.'

'Did you go out again that night?'

'No - although I don't have any witnesses.'

As expected, Professor Castletons story checked out.

He had been with Aunty Lydia much of the afternoon.
Heather and Isaac had seen Sarah arrive and leave the professor's office in the morning. Yes, the Professor had left around
midday as Isaac was heading out to pick up some lunch and
yes he did return about 4 and leave again shortly after. Sarah
wasn't there at all during that time and anyway she couldn't
have gotten into the building without pressing the security but-
ton - which she never did. Before Heather left at 7pm she had
taken some rubbish to the bins out the back and there were no
cars parked there then.

A doorknock near the Professor's home confirmed that a
neighbor walking her dog about 8.30pm that night, noticed
lights on in his house. The garage door was down so she

couldn't swear he was home - but she could hear music coming from inside.

They stayed in Mt Isa all the next day quizzing Health Food Stores and Pharmacies. Sarah had been to quite a number of them, comparing products and looking for advice. In the end she'd gone with the brand that had the most positive reviews. No one thought she showed any signs of being worried or upset - except maybe a little frustrated at all the natural options there were out there.

The pathologist's report indicated that the post mortem bruising that had occurred suggested it was the result of pushing and pulling rather than holding her down. "So we are back to a single assailant again I think. We'll know more when the toxicology tests come back.'

Amongst all this bad news, something positive arrives. Lily Fernandez' father and sister have provided DNA and we should finally have an answer. How quickly will depend on those strings that need to be pulled in Manila.

✦

6

'Of course this could be a copycat killing.'

Nina Forde was not totally convinced this was the work of the same killer. It was more brutal, the car had been left - not destroyed or hidden and it was very close to a main highway with a steady stream of traffic. The car was facing into Mt Isa rather than home to Cloncurry. And the murder weapon was right there. It's never been left at any of the other sites. The only things that make it appear the same, are the facial injuries.....and maybe the mystery escape. How did he get away?'

Jules tapped her fingers on her notepad.

'You could be right. Could be a copycat although we've never released information about the head injury beyond blunt force trauma. It would have to be someone really in the know to copy the facial injury so exactly down the left hand side of her face and head. I have been thinking though - about what my pathologist said. - At first he thought two people were involved. I know he is now saying well maybe not.. but what if his first thoughts were right? What if there are two people. One to dispose of the body, and the other one to wait nearby and pick them up. It would explain a lot - not just about this murder, but the others as well."

Jack Harding sank his face into his hands. 'Fuck. I don't even want to think about it. Two of the bastards instead of one. It's already a nightmare. Fucking hell.'

Then he looked up. 'Sorry for the language. I'm just so.....'
He shook his head in exasperation. "But I'll tell you what.....the
cricket bat and everything - that tells me this wasn't a planned
murder. He's just used whatever was there to kill her. And on
the highway there it would have been too risky to set fire to the
car - besides he - or they - didn't need to. I'll bet we won't find
a thing in it.

Two days later Sarah's body was released to her family. The
last secret it gave up was that the substance in her stomach was
an unidentified but quite toxic anion, which probably would
have eventually led to her death if the cricket bat hadn't gotten
there first. She would have been in a great deal of pain though,
and maybe unconscious. Certainly too ill to resist.

The car, just as Jack Harding had predicted, didn't provide
anything that could help identify the killer. Thanks to the fastidious way Sarah maintained it, the only DNA and fingerprints
found belonged to her family and one of the young female store
assistants she often gave a lift home to if they worked late. There
were some unknown fingerprints on the bonnet and the boot
latch but nothing they could get a match with. Both the drivers
and passenger side doors had been wiped clean. He - or they
- didn't make any obvious mistakes. Even the cricket kit was
unhelpful. Jess confirmed that it belonged to him. He'd left it
on the back seat of the car when Sarah had picked him up from
cricket practice the night before she was killed. It would have
been unzipped because he'd been in a rush and just chucked
everything in. So the killer merely needed to reach in and take
out the bat. The handle was covered with Jess's prints and one
or two of Nick's. Clearly gloves had been worn by the killer
because there was a lot of smudging. The rest of the bat had
Jess's prints here and there but was covered in blood and some
dust from the site. Grass fragments in the toe of the bat were
most likely from local cricket pitches.

Ray knew Sarah had gone to Mt Isa on 'women's business,' but he assumed she was seeing a specialist. Her menopausal problems had gone beyond the joke of 'hot flushes.'

'Some days you'd be walking on eggshells all day. Say the slightest thing to upset her and she'd be off. Either raging or bawling her eyes out. Then she'd calm down and get upset all over again for being such a bitch. It was tough on us all, tougher on her though. None of the doctors here would give her hormones because her mother, aunty, sister they all died of ovarian cancer quite young. I thought she'd gone to see a woman's doctor in Isa to see what her options were. What a waste, I still can't believe it....me and the boys....it's hard.. .... The sooner you catch the bastard who did this the better.'

On the day of Sarah's funeral, a freak storm hit just about the time she was about to be buried. It didn't stop people turning up though. Most of the town was there as well as friends from surrounding districts. The whole place was a sea of umbrellas which gave it an almost surreal appearance. Professor Castleton had come out of respect too and stayed to offer his deepest condolences to Ray. Jack Harding looked around the crowd for someone who didn't belong, but they were all people he was familiar with, except for her relatives from Ipswich and Ray vouched for them. None had been around when Sarah had been murdered. As people drifted away, they dragged mud and slush on their shoes creating a sad brown river along the pathway that only came to an end when it reached the grass area. By the next day, the mud had dried to a dirty red, like old blood. The caretaker came by and hosed it away.

It was only a little over a month later when the DNA samples taken from Lily Fernandez' family came back as a positive match.

For Lily's family, the news was a tragedy but for Jules and the team working on the case in Hughenden, it was the best news they could have hoped for. At last something to work with. Jack Harding headed off to Manoora with Senior Constable Forde. They took with them copies of the photo of Lily with the older man and of items from her box of personal possessions - the crucifix and the rosary. While they were investigating the situation in Manoora, Jules Banyenan had flown down to Adelaide to interview Cheryl Hinkler again. She'd negotiated a small reward for Cheryl for helping to identify Lily and promised she'd get the lot if it led to the murderer.

Cheryl was pleased... but not pleased. $10,000 was a lot better than the nothing she had now, but the rest of the reward was just a pie-in-the-sky promise. Jules Banyenan reminded Cheryl that they still had no proof that Lily's murder was connected to the other cases - 'but we have an excellent team working on it.'

Now she wanted Cheryl to think back about any details she might have missed. 'Who was the man she fancied? Did she ever come home with any signs of violence? Anything you might have missed before?' She hoped the promise of another $90,000 might jog her memory.

Cheryl was flattered that she was considered an important person in the investigation. It was the only time in her adult life that anyone had shown her any respect and she was keen to remain a part of Lily's story for as long as possible.

'It definitely wasn't the man in that photo - that was from before she turned up in Manoora. What can I tell you? Well, she was very religious you know. When the priest came to town she'd go to the mass - ask God to forgive all her sins before she repeated them all over again. As I said before. She wasn't her normal self for a week or so before she went missing. something was bugging her.'

Jules tried to suggest some lines of thought.

'She might have seen something …you know …something she shouldn't have - or someone from before. Did she have friends? '

'..Well we were sorta friends….helped each other when we could, but I've already told ya - she didn't tell me anything like that.'

After thinking for a minute though, something did come to mind.

'Yeah…..early on, there was this other woman working at the pub she made friends with - spoke the same language - Frida her name was…she worked in the kitchen - but she left there pretty quick with a truckie she picked up with. That was a couple of months before Lily disappeared……What else can I tell you..? Well she got a lot of calls that she didn't answer. One of the girls showed her how to block numbers you don't wanna get….and after that she got almost no calls. She didn't call many people either. Mostly texted. Those fingers would fly across the letters. Dunno how she did it with those long nails of hers. There's nothin' else I can say. Maybe if you find the arse-hole who did this I might be able to identify him. He must have lived or worked in Manoora hey?'

As she rose to leave, something made Jules Banyenan ask one more question. "What was the name of the priest?'

'Buggered if I know…..Ask Dave from the pub. They used to hold the mass in the pub's dining room.'

Jules was immediately on the phone to Jack Harding.

'I need you to track down the priest who used to visit Manoora at the time Lily was working there. Dave from the pub will know his name. Lily used to confess to him every time he was there.'

'Dave - yeah I know him. I think he owns the place. I'll find out about the priest but it doesn't matter what she's confessed to him, he's not going to tell you is he.'

Jack paused for a second. '.... oh wait..you're not thinking he's a suspect are you?'

'No..... just a person I'd like to talk to at this stage.'

In Manoora, there was a palpable sense of relief that Lily had been identified. Everyone saw this as the first step to catching the killer even though there was still no firm evidence that this killing was related to the others.

Most of the people who'd been in the town for 6 or 7 years recognised Lily. - Not that there were that many of them. Plus there had been a lot of fly-in-fly-out workers through around that time. Everyone of those would need to be interviewed. After some initial back and forth and checking with company solicitors, the Wolfram Bowenfield Mine agreed to provide a list of previous employees. It was Nina and Turley's job to contact every one of them. Over half were no longer at their last known address - their details would be sent to Brisbane to chase up. A few were deceased, two were in jail, and the rest were happy to talk to Nina. All the men they did manage to speak to denied having anything to do with any of the women, claiming they were 'happily married', or 'don't do that stuff.'

Dave did indeed know the priest. He wasn't at all religious but his wife was and it was her idea to organize his regular visits. Father Mulcahy was the name of the priest and he used to stop in twice a month to hold a mass and sometimes baptize or marry someone. Mostly Koa people from around here who'd been converted. 'I often used to think gees, why would they do that? What good's the church ever done them?' He shook his head in disbelief.

Father Mulcahy was already 'getting on a bit 'at the time and had moved to Mt Isa permanently a couple of years ago when the driving became too much for him.

'So he's still in the area then?

'Oh yes, and alive and well from what I understand.'

Dave was even more helpful when it came to information about Lily.

'She used to hang out with this bloke - big, muscular guy - good looking according to the girls - spoke with a foreign accent, Russian, Polish...I dunno - something like that. What was his name? (he called out to his wife) .....Bodgy...yeah that was it Bodgy. She was all over him like a rash and I think he took advantage.'

'Did you ever see him hit her or threaten her.'

'No nothing like that...I think he just got what he wanted without paying. '

'Is he still around?"

'No..long gone...long gone.

'Did he leave around the same time as Lily?'

'Mate..you're talking about something that happened years ago. They come, they go - I don't really pay that much attention. The mine people could tell you that.'

Back in Hughenden, Nina Forde looked down the list of employees from the time and noted that 'Bodgy' was likely to be Bojan Katic, a Serbian national who had worked at the mine for 6 months before quitting suddenly for - supposedly - a better job in the Pilbara in Western Australia. Talking to a few of the other employees who were there at the time, she confirmed Bojan's nickname was indeed Bodgy. Everyone said pretty much the same thing about him. He was loud, friendly and popular with the ladies. No one remembered him as the least bit violent. Just the opposite. When he'd had a few too many he tended to sing bad 70's disco songs and imitate John Tavolta's moves from Saturday Night Fever. He was a man who apparently always steered clear of trouble. Still he would have to be tracked down and questioned.

Father Mulcahy was easier to find. His eyesight had started to deteriorate a few years back and he was now legally blind. He was living in a Catholic aged care place - 'In God's waiting room' he joked, with a number of older nuns and a very old priest who slept most of the day.

'It's a tragedy what happened to Lily. Heartbreaking. Still at least finding her will give her family some closure. I must say though - I am surprised the family had never tried to find her. She used to send them money you know. I'm happy to talk to you about her in general - anything that might help you, but I can't share anything she told me in confidence. What I will say is she was very, very conflicted. She'd been raised in a very traditional, religious family in the Philippines - went to mass every week - sometimes more than once....and now she found herself working ....well as a prostitute to put it bluntly. She was very afraid her family would find out and so she'd cut off all contact. I think she always hoped that she'd find a way out into a normal life again, but she had problems with her visa. Her biggest fear was getting caught and sent back - so she dropped out of the system.'

'Why was she afraid of being sent back?'

"I don't know..something she witnessed I think - or someone she knew - I told her she should apply for refugee status, but it was too late...her solicitor said they wouldn't believe her without some pretty strong evidence. You should ask her family, they might know. '

'Anything else?'

'Nothing I can talk about.'

'Anything that could get her killed?'

'I wouldn't have thought so - but it's a rough world she found herself in, so who knows.'

Jack Harding called Jules Banyenan. 'I think you can cross Father Mulcahy off the list of suspects. He's almost blind. '

'We'll leave him there for the moment - for Lily's death.'

'OK, but I think this Bodgy guy is a more likely candidate.'

'Maybe, we'll know more when we find him.'

Jules Banyenan arranged a zoom meeting to go over all the new information.

'I think our best bet is to find Bojan Katic - although if he is still in the Pilbara, he certainly can't be linked to any of the other deaths. Then there's the problem that Lily appeared to be running away from. We'll contact her family and see if they can help. But if it was a 'hit' from someone in her past, it's not going to be connected to the other murders. The only other Philippines national out there was a woman named Frida who'd left town long before Lily disappeared and we've had no success finding her. I think we should still keep looking though, she was supposed to have been friendly with Lily, but she could have passed her whereabouts onto someone she shouldn't have.'

None of them wanted to consider the possibility that Lily's death was totally unrelated to the other murders, especially Nina.

'I can't believe these four deaths aren't connected. I mean - they've all got the same head injuries - what's the chance of that happening by accident. Especially as out here, the usual way to murder someone is to shoot them.

✧

7

Just 10 days after Lilly had been identified, local Cloncurry butcher Geoff Baxter was dropping off an order to one of his most valued customers. Christine 'Chrissie' Gleeson was the owner and chef of 'The Clon Cafe - which had become a bit of a foodie hub in the area. Chrissie Gleeson had made a point of promoting native Australian ingredients in her recipes and had become very good friends with a couple of Pitta Pitta Aunties who used to advise her on their uses.

Chrissie and the Aunties would regularly go out on foraging trips. Twice a year she'd hold special banquets to promote these ingredients and the events were so popular that people came from as far away as Brisbane. As a result she was prominently featured in local tourist brochures and social media. Suppliers such as local butcher Geoff Baxter benefitted by association. If his meat was good enough for her, it was good enough for them. So when she rang through an order at 6pm and asked if she could have it early the next morning he was happy to help.

When he arrived, it was just after 7am. The town's early risers were on the move, but it was still pretty quiet. Geoff Baxter knocked on the door but Chrissie didn't answer. He peeked through the glass window and could see a light coming from the kitchen and further back in the storage area. Her car was parked in the lane way so he knew she was there.

When she didn't answer the door after he'd knocked a few times, he tried the back door - it was unlocked - so he stepped in calling out her name at the same time. Just to the left was a cool room. It was wide open and the alarm was giving off a gentle 'Beep, beep,' as a reminder to close the door. As he turned to look inside - expecting to see Chrissie making room for his delivery, he could see what looked like blood on the floor. A step closer and the horror of it hit him. She was on her back, but barely recognisable. The left hand side of her face had been caved in. Geoff's hands were shaking so hard he couldn't get them to push the right numbers on the phone, so he jumped in his car and drove around the corner to the local police station.

Constable Meryl Jackson grabbed some crime scene tape and she and Geoff drove back to the cafe. It was still exactly as he had left it.

Jules Banyenan was just about to jump into the shower, when her phone rang. The screen identified the caller as Cloncurry Police. She'd better take it.

'Jules Banyenan.'

'Constable Jackson from Cloncurry here. .....ah...I think *we've* got one now.'

'Got a what?'

'A murder like the two in Hughenden and that one in Mt Isa.. you know....like Sarah Newhouse and the others. Same kind of wounds anyway. Her name is Chrissie Gleeson and she's a bit of a legend up here - runs a foodie cafe. The butcher found her in the kitchen. My senior said I should call you right away.'

Within 90 minutes Jules and the same team involved in the investigation of Sarah's death were on their way.

Constable Jackson had only made one call - to Jules Banyenan to report the murder, but by the time she'd set up the crime scene perimeter, a local doctor had arrived to make some observations on behalf of the pathologist. He'd been given instructions from the team in the helicopter as to what exactly was required.

And as if by magic Aunty Kath and Aunty June had turned up and begun mourning rituals for their good friend.

Geoff was still sitting on the front steps of the cafe in a state of suspended animation when Jack Harding and Nina Forde also arrived and joined the Cloncurry Police team. By now a steady stream of locals had made their way to the cafe to have a squiz. Jack and Nina moved them back and suggested they all go home and let the police do their work. There was a bit of confusion and anger over whether Geoff was a witness or the perpetrator, but once that was sorted out, the people calmed down and began to drift away.

When Jules and her team touched down, it appeared the town had come to a complete standstill. Everything was open, but nothing was moving. As the pathologist and forensics team got on with their work, Jules sought out Geoff. He didn't think there was anything more he could add to the picture that he hadn't already told the police, but he went over the details again for Jules.

'She was just her normal self when she phoned through the order last night. Not upset or anything - she said she'd be here by 7am this morning and she wanted the Lamb delivered by 7.30. I left my shop at about 7, so I would have got here a few minutes later. No one answered but I could see lights on round the back. Her car was here - that's it there - so I went round the back. The door was unlocked, I called out, went in and there she was. I nearly shat myself. I mean I'm a butcher, used to seeing blood, but not like that. Before I saw her face, I thought maybe she'd had an accident - tripped and fallen, but geez......I tried to call the police but I couldn't get the phone to work, so I drove there. Luckily there was some-one on duty.

He couldn't remember seeing anyone or hearing anything - there was a truck passing through from Isa but it turned straight onto the Flinders highway.

Besides the shock of finding a valued customer bludgeoned to death, he had a real concern that he was going to be blamed for it. He was mumbling to himself about where the police might find his fingerprints. 'I knocked on the front door and maybe touched the handle...and I definitely touched the glass window on the left with my hands and forehead when I tried to see inside and I opened the backdoor so I must have touched that too.' He was pretty certain he hadn't touched anything else - 'well maybe the coolroom door - but that's it. '

Jules asked him if the killer could still have been there - hid-ing in another part of the cafe.

'Bloody hell, I hope not - but I don't remember hearing any-thing. What am I going to do? - people think I did it.'

'I think we've cleared that up. But look - you're very upset, why don't I get someone to drive you home. You can pick up your van later.'

'No..there's over $500 dollars worth of lamb in that van. It's already been sitting here for a couple of hours. - I'm taking it straight back to the shop. I'll be ok, it's just down the road.'

'We'll probably need to talk to you again later when we have more information about how and when she died - and we'll also need to take your prints for elimination purposes - but don't worry, we're not considering you a suspect - your clothes are too clean. The killer would be spattered with blood.'

Geoff gave a sort of half pleased smile and got up to walk towards his truck. Two steps and his legs wobbled under him. Someone in the crowd - a regular customer of Geoffs, offered to drive Geoff and his truck full of lamb back to the shop where his apprentice could help unload it.

In the midst of all the activity, Nina Forde walked across to the two Aunties to have a quiet word. She'd been at school for a time with Aunty Kath's granddaughter Emily and so was not a total stranger. The two Aunties said they had never witnessed any trouble when they went foraging together with Chrissie. Often they were the only ones there. But Chrissie did sometimes go out on her own. The two women sat quietly for a while, before Auntry June dragged a memory back from some time ago.

'Long time back - she mentioned she saw something on her own with them glasses she always had with her. Maybe she saw, maybe she didn't, so she said nothing. That's all.'

Nina thanked the Aunties for their help and took the opportunity to ask after Emily. It turned out that she was a qualified early childhood teacher and working in a kindergarten in Mt Isa. Aunty Kath was very proud of her, but hoped that she would soon return to put her learning to good use in the local community.

Nina gave Aunty Kath a card with her mobile number on it. 'Please pass this on to Emily. I'd love to catch up for a coffee next time she's in town.'

Allowing for the fact that her body was found in the doorway of the coolroom, the pathologist's initial estimate of time of death was between 11.30pm and 12.30am the night before. Plenty of time for the killer to get away to anywhere. And at that time of night, there wouldn't have been too many people walking the streets of Cloncurry.

Unlike the previous victims, Chrissie had been left where she fell, not posed like Adele, Amy, or Sarah Newhouse, who had even had her hands placed back on the steering wheel and her seatbelt buckled up.

There was a murder weapon however - two actually. Both indicated this was an unplanned spur of the moment killing, so it had something in common with Sarah's death. Chrissie had been struck on the back of the head with a meat cleaver which had been dropped to the side of the coolroom door. The forensic report suggested that before she fell, she probably turned to see her assailant who had grabbed a small fire extinguisher from off the wall and whacked her across the left side of her face with it.

Both weapons had been cleaned of prints but there were lots of traces of her smeared blood. The killer was likely spattered with blood and it would have been all over his shoes. He'd actually stepped in blood but had used kitchen paper to try and clean them up, leaving bits of shoe prints on the paper too. Geoff might also have stepped in the blood without realizing it, as there seemed to be different prints in different sizes. The forensics team were hoping that in the sea of partial footprints they'd recovered from the site there was at least one clear set that had been accidentally left behind by the killer.

Over the next day or so, everyone who'd ever been in the back of the cafe came forward to get their prints taken. Geoff's as expected showed up on the front and back door, the back door handle, a glass panel by the front door, on a wall next to the coolroom (he'd probably braced himself there after the shock discovery) and on the coolroom door. There was also a slight trace of Chrissie's blood on the sole of one of the shoes he was wearing at the time, which matched with the one print of his shoe found at the scene. Small traces of blood on one trouser leg were identified as animal blood. He was not a suspect.

The common thread that ran through the testimony of everyone that came forward was that Chrissie was a popular and well liked person. She had bought something positive to the community and even the old die-hards who thought her food was a bit of a gimmick, appreciated she'd livened the place up a bit. After a week or so of collecting prints from the locals, there were still a large number that couldn't be eliminated, but who knew how long they'd been there?

The pathologists report stated that Chrissie was a 54 woman with no underlying health issues.

The wound to the back of her head had caused significant damage and bleeding to the back of her skull, but it was the blunt force trauma to the front of her head that caused the massive brain bleed that killed her. Some defensive wounds to both arms suggested that she was conscious for long enough after the initial attack to try to fend off the second-ary attack. But there were no signs of a struggle. The fact that she'd had her back to her assailant to begin with sug-gested she knew them and didn't regard them as a threat. She'd probably turned and hit the ground instantly - and then instinctively put up her arms to protect herself. Blood tests would be carried out but only really to find out if she had consumed enough alcohol for it to have affected her ability to react. There was an open bottle of red wine on the benchtop in the kitchen with only her prints on the bottle -and just one glass - again with only her prints on it. But the dishwasher was filled with clean dishes so it was hard to know if there had been a second glass.

Gabrielle, who worked at the cafe as a waitress, had walked through the place with Jules Banyenan and spotted nothing out of the ordinary,

"Last orders were taken at 9.00 on weeknights, so the place was empty by 10.30. Last night was a bit quieter and I finished just before 10. Usually I would stay and help her clean up but she told me to go - that I could come in a half hour earlier tomorrow to reset the tables.

I didn't get the impression she was expecting anyone - she sometimes did that if it was quiet - sent me home and cleaned up herself. She reckoned that's when she did her best thinking - when she was alone there at night. But I think someone did pull up as I was driving away. I didn't see who. A light coloured 4 wheel drive. I didn't pay any attention really. Just saw it in my rear view mirror as I was driving off- so it must have been coming from Isa direction, not Richmond.'

As expected, Gabrielle's prints had been found all over the place in the cafe but she was not a suspect. In fact she'd provided the first important piece of information they'd had since the murder. The killer may have arrived at about 10pm and was driving from the direction of Mt Isa in a light coloured 4WD. I was something to get on with.

Before she flew back to Brisbane Jules drove across to Hughenden for a catch up with Jack Harding. Out came the whiteboard again and Chrissie Gleeson's details were added. They all felt the differences between this murder and the others showed there was something else at play but they were certain it was related.

Nina recounted the Aunty's story about Chrissie maybe seeing something when she was out foraging. The glasses, which Nina had initially thought were reading glasses, turned out to be binoculars, found on the front seat of her car. So as vague as the information was, 'seeing something' might certainly provide a powerful motive for killing her.

By the end of the discussion, all three were working on the hypothesis that Chrissie had thought she had spotted someone she recognized at one of the murder scenes. She hadn't said anything at the time because she wasn't sure. But maybe after Sarah's death she mentioned her suspicions to the killer - then it all came to a head and he panicked and killed her. It was a solid theory, but it meant the killer was well known to her. Maybe a regular customer, supplier, someone else in the hospitality business. A friend even. Jack and Nina would get onto this line of enquiry right away.

Back in Brisbane, word came through that Lily's family had no real idea what she had been afraid of, although when she left, there'd been a lot of drug related shootings happening, some of people she knew. But her sister suggested that 'Maybe she was afraid of coming home and facing her family.' That was all they'd say. They did not want her remains and meager belongings returned, but wondered at the chance of some sort of financial compensation. Jules passed the request on to another department. She had more important things to do.

Because the murders of Sarah Newhouse and Christine Gleeson took place just weeks apart, there was a general sense of both fear and optimism amongst the investigation team. Fear because perhaps the killer was getting bolder and certainly more reckless. Optimism because this latest murder at least suggested Chrissie was killed for what she had seen or heard. She was the key. Perhaps the Aunties too - but they'd have to be careful about involving them. The last thing they wanted was more victims murdered to protect the killer's identity.

8

Over in Kalgoorlie, Bojan 'Bodgy' Katic was surprised to get an early morning visit from the local police.

They were friendly enough, 'Just making a few general enquiries about a woman named Lily Fernandez.' They showed him a photo. It took him a few seconds to adjust to the sunlight, 'Oh yeah..I know her ...from Manoora.'

'Did you have any relationship with her?'

He smiled. 'Just for pleasure...not business. She's a Kurva.... you know..for money. But for me it was free.'

'So when did you last see her?"

'Years ago. Let me think....maybe 5 - maybe 6 years ago...I left Manoora to come first to the Pilbara, then Meekatharra then here.'

'Why did you leave?'

'Better money here. Better life.'

'Who left first - you or Miss Fernandez.'

'Me. I stopped things with her - then a couple of weeks later I leave.'

'Why did you stop things with her?'

'Why are you asking me all these things?'

'She's been found murdered. Well her remains have been found. She's apparently been deceased for a number of years.'

'That's a sad thing. But these things happen to those kinds of women.'

'You haven't answered my question. Why did you stop things with her?'

Bodgy rubbed the last of the sleep from his eyes.

'She was trouble. She said she was going to be a mama - that it was my baby. I told her best thing is to get rid of it. It's not my baby, I don't want a baby- especially I don't want a baby with you. She was crying and saying what a good catholic girl she was and that she could never do that. 'God would never forgive me' she said. She wanted me to marry her. I told her - You're crazy. You go with many men, how do you know who is the father? Why would I marry someone like her? I told her to piss off - find someone else to trick into marrying her.'

'Did you see her after that?'

'Nah, but she kept calling and leaving messages. Crying and begging. I could see she was going to cause me trouble so I left.'

'You didn't hit her or anything when she was asking you to marry her?'

'Hit her? First I don't hit women. Second, I don't hit a woman having a baby. I don't hit men either. Ask the people here. I don't get into fights with anyone. I'm what you say? - a lover not a fighter.'

'Well we'll need a list of the places where you've worked since arriving in W.A. okay.'

'Sure.' He wrote down the names in his funny backhanded writing.'

'Ah...a fellow lefty.'

'What?'

'You're left handed.'

'Yeah...my parents tried to forbid it..where I come from, you should only write with your right hand, or the devil will catch you. But I use which hand I want. That's old nana tradition anyway. '

The Kalgoorlie police sent back a report on Bojan Katic which suggested he certainly had a motive to kill Lily, but... ....'the information you gave us seemed to suggest the killer is right handed. Bojan is left-handed. Also he freely admitted he had been in a sexual relationship with her and he broke it off because she claimed she was pregnant and wanted him to marry her. He didn't believe (or wouldn't admit) it was his child and told her in his words, 'to piss off' and then got as far away from her as quickly as he could. His alibi checks out too. He's been here for 5 1/2 years. Never left the region in all that time, so there's no way he could be involved in the others.'

Pregnant. That was new.

'Would you say the killer is left handed?" It was a question Jules posed to Professor Castleton, Mark Simpson, who examined the skeleton and the current team of pathologists.

They all replied back almost instantly in the following order.

"Possible but not likely.'

'No'.

And 'The evidence suggests a right handed assailant'.

Bojan was off the list and the skeleton was once again added to the current list of victims.

Christine Gleeson's remains had been returned to her family in Sydney for cremation, but she was too important to the town for her death to go unmarked. The Cloncurry Council voted to hold a public memorial service in her honor one month from now, when the shock of her murder was not quite as raw. The plans quickly morphed into a celebration of her life and legacy with a number of restaurants and cafes in the region offering to create a food 'wake' to follow the memorial service.

Aunty Kath and Aunty June were brought into the town under the pretext of getting their advice on the menu, as well as providing some funny anecdotes for the memorial. They were not comfortable about being a part of the service, but they did want to attend out of respect. Jules had asked Nina to get some more details about those foraging trips, so she sat down with a pot of sweet tea and their favorite Anzac biscuits and just chatted about this and that. Gradually this and that also included Chrissie, and then the field trips. Then the field trips included information that she always had her special glasses with her, 'mostly looking for birds and animals. She was learning about this country. Nice lady that Chrissie. Always did the right thing with the foods. Never took too much. '

'So what do you think she saw?'

'Don't know for sure. We weren't there that time. But it was that day the car blew up down Hughenden way....You know the one. She was telling us about the fire...and then she got a bit upset. Whatever she saw - she didn't like it. But she didn't tell us what.'

'You didn't ask?'

'Not our business.'

'Well it's a good idea not to mention this to anyone else. What she saw might be why she's dead. Wouldn't want anything to happen to you.'

After a bit more conversation about the general state of things in the community Nina left them to finish their tea and biscuits and sent off her report to Jules Banyenan. She added that she planned to take a pair of binoculars out the area where Amy's body had been found and look for likely places where Chrissie might have been foraging, then she'd use the binoculars to see what was visible. If she could find out where Chrissie had been that morning, she might be able to discover what or who she had seen. It was a long shot but you never know - 'If I have to, I'll do it in my own time - I think Senior Sergeant Harding will help too.'

Jules was pleased that Nina was prepared to go above and beyond. Country police can be a bit hit and miss. These two were hits - even Constable Turley whatever his name was, was promising.

Jules organized a zoom meeting that involved the Brisbane, Hughenden, Winton, Cloncurry and Mt Isa Police.

'We now have some important new pieces of evidence that could help move this case forward. Firstly, according to Bojan Katic who is no longer a suspect, Lily was pregnant. I think Winton police need to get onto this, see if you can find out who the father could have been if it wasn't Mr Katic. Dave or his wife might have an idea. I'll give Cheryl Hinkler a call in Adelaide and see what she knows. Not expecting much from her though. We've interviewed her twice and she's never mentioned the pregnancy - and I think she would have if she'd known anything about it, she really wants the reward money.'

Detective Sergeant Crossly from Mt Isa butted in. "I understand why this Katic bloke is off the suspect list for the recent murders - but couldn't he still be responsible for Lily Fernandez?"

'No, he's left handed - the damage done to her head and face - and to all the other victims, appears to have been inflicted by a right handed person.'

For a few minutes various officers on the zoom call tried to imagine swinging a heavy object with their right hand, then with their left. They weren't totally convinced.

Jules took back control of the meeting.

'Don't waste your time. Only Sarah was hit by a bat from the front....and as for Chrissie Gleeson, the angle of the meat cleaver on the back of her head also says right handed. And if the killer was left handed, when he picked up the fire extinguisher he would have swung it from the left..(she made a one handed swinging motion) So just take it from me - well actually from all the pathologists involved - all the evidence points to a right handed person.

Now DS Crossley, we have a few important tasks for Mt Isa police to attend to as well. Firstly, have another word with Father Mulcahy. He'll say he can't tell you anything - but see if you can get a feel for whether Lily had spoken to him about the baby. According to Mr Katic, she didn't believe in abortion..... so send a woman out - someone sympathetic who might get him on side. I'd also like someone there to have another chat with Aunty Lydia. Find out if she had any dealings with Christine Gleeson. Did she take her out foraging too? Did she ever see anything strange when she was out and about there? And maybe walk the route Sarah took from the chemist shops to Professor Castletons place to see if there's any cameras we missed.'

D.S Crossly thought this might be a waste of time. 'They'd be taped over by now wouldn't they?'

'Probably, but not all systems work like that. Look, we're desperate here folks. I feel like we're just one clue away from finding Lily Fernandez' killer and one step away from finding Christine Gleesons killer ... and I'm damn sure they are both the same person that killed the other three women. So go back and talk to Chrissie's friends and the people who were there that night. One of them knows something, they probably just don't realize it. That's it for now - except Jack can you stay on the line, I'd like to talk to you about that map you're putting together.'

'Sure, I'll get Nina too. She's put a lot of effort into this.'

Everyone else signed off - leaving just Jack, Nina and Jules and her team.

'OK what have you got for me?'

Jack angled the camera up to a map pinned to the wall. It was shaded in different colors and there were a number of drawing pins dotted here and there.

Jack spoke while Nina pointed out the various features.

'OK so here's the road out of Hughenden and this is where it turns off to the dirt tracks. The green pin here is the shack where the body was found- but it's since been pulled down - and the orange pins are other outbuildings or old shacks. Now these black pins show the route Dr Sidowski jogged along - the double black pin there is where he was when he saw the car go up in flames. On the way up to the hill he didn't see Chrissie - we've double checked that - didn't see her ute either - which he would have recognized because it has Cafe Clon painted on the side. So she was definitely not parked anywhere around there.

When he got up to the top of the hill, he looked in the direction of the burning car and the house. He was too far away to see what was happening, but he says he didn't see anyone anywhere. So all this area to the north of the shack is coloured grey. That means we don't think Chrissie was there. Also I think if she had been over here to the east - he would have seen her as he turned on the track - like this - (Nina points in the direction). So that's pink. Still possible but unlikely. No, most likely she was here in the south - or over here in the east - in the same direction as Dr Sidowski.'

'You're not suggesting Dr Sidowski…?'

'No, no…we went back over all our early notes and Dr Sidowski actually mentioned that a couple of days after we found Amy's body, Chrissie called him to ask if he had seen anyone out there. He thought it was just general curiosity and we didn't think anything of it either. But knowing what we know now, I think she might have thought he'd seen whatever it was that she'd seen. Anyway there's a bit of a rise over here to the east that goes down here to the south. There's a small stream down there and as he came down the hill towards the burning car, Dr Sidowski would have had a good view of it. And if she was over here - (he points to the pink section of the map) she would have seen that area too. Only problem is, Dr Sidowski was totally focussed on the burning car. Just the same, we're drawing up a grid from there, right up to the top of that rise and we'll check it out square by square. Any foot or tyre prints will be long gone of course but there might be something. He would have to have gotten out of there in a real hurry and could have dropped something along the way. - the car keys for instance - we never found those. It will take us a while, but it's worth doing.'

'Keep me in touch - and thanks for this.'

The weeks passed by. Despite some sensitive questioning by Senior Constable Marnie Chan, Father Mulcahy would reveal nothing that Lily Fernandez had spoken to him about - he wouldn't even acknowledge that he knew she was pregnant. But he did repeat something he'd said the first time he was interviewed. 'She was conflicted.' That suggested to Marnie Chan that he did know, and that she was thinking of having a termination.

The police in Winton hadn't been able to find a doctor or nurse who had ever seen her as a patient, or any records that she'd ever sought medical attention from any health professional in the area. She'd probably self-diagnosed her pregnancy with a kit - and if she was going to have a termination, the nearest hospital she could rely on was in Isa. But as far as anyone knew, she hadn't left Manoora since arriving and this is where her body was found. There was also the issue of her immigration status. She had no medicare card and only showed her passport when she absolutely had to - being careful to keep her thumb over the expired visa date. A hospital would not fall for that. As for other possible 'fathers', well Dave and his wife were really the only ones still left in the town who knew her at all and they had no idea beyond Bodgy. 'She was a sex worker, so it could have been anyone.'

Cheryl, as expected, knew nothing about the baby. 'I knew something was up but she didn't say anything. Are you sure it's true? She didn't seem to be sick or anything.'

Jules got the impression that Cheryl was a bit hurt about not being let in on the secret - worse - not being asked to help. At the end of the call she asked Jules if she was any closer to getting the rest of the reward money.

"We still haven't found the killer Cheryl, so if you think of anything else - give me a call.'

Aunty Lydia was not much help either. She'd never gone out foraging with Chrissie and had only met her once when she was negotiating the supply of some ingredients with a local grower. She hadn't often gone foraging with the Professor either. Once.. or maybe twice - like when she found the lime trees, she'd shown him places to look, but she was only recently back on talking terms with him.

'Once I caught him you know - he just went out and picked some women's medicine.. Didn't ask, just helped himself. I told him you might be a big time expert but this is a women's place. You don't go out there again or I'll make big trouble for you. If you want something - ask me and I might help or I might not. I put a big scare up him and I made him donate some money to the women's shelter to make up for it. After that, he always asked.'

'So you and the Professor are now friends?'

'I wouldn't say he's a friend. He 's always looking for different kinds of medicines to write about in a book. I only tell him things he's allowed to know. But the lime trees were different. They don't grow out here naturally. One of them old cameleers must have planted them. They were in a different place - not near the women's place. He could have those. That's why I took him out there that day - you know when that other woman was killed.'

Marnie Chan thanked Aunty Lydia, but then she had a last minute thought. 'Aunty Lydia, did anyone ever ask you...about medicine to get rid of a baby?'

Aunty looked shocked. "Why would someone do that?'

'I was just curious because you mentioned women's medicine.'

'That's not what it's for.'

'OK..thanks for your help.'

Meanwhile Nina Forde had asked the same question of Aunty Kath and Aunty June and the reaction was the same.

'Even if someone asked us, we wouldn't say anything. We don't want that kind of trouble around here. No,.... your mob has doctors for that.'

Over the next 2 weeks, Nina and Jack Harding meticulously went over all the possible places Christine Gleeson could have been on the morning Amy Moreno's body was found. In the end they found one likely spot about 500 meters from the shack. There were a lot of native orchids growing there and that would have appealed to Chrissie. It wasn't exactly open country - there were a lot of scrappy ironbarks and shrubs growing, but it was on a bit of a ridge and if you scanned the area with binoculars, you would have had a good view of an overgrown track that ran behind the shack where Amy was found. The shack itself was hidden by trees - but a possible getaway route could be clearly seen.

As Nina said in her report to Jules Banyenan. 'If she heard the explosion and quickly looked through her binoculars to

see what was going on, she would have been able to see anyone getting away along the back track. From the top of the hill
where Dr Sidowski turned back, he would have been able to see
the same area - if he'd looked - although possibly he would have
been a bit far away. Anyway we've searched all around that
area and there's nothing. I guess we were being a bit optimistic
thinking that after all this time we'd somehow find something
none of the previous searches had found.'

Jules thanked her for all her hard work, but they both knew
this information would only become useful once they had a
suspect. Nevertheless, it went up on the whiteboard and into
the file.

9

Jules Banyenan logged onto her computer. It was now 1 year exactly since Christine Gleesons body had been found.

Never had so many scenarios come to nothing.

Her inbox was filled with the usual updates on current cases, including the weekly note from Amy Moreno's family asking if there was any further news. It was always painful to answer that 'the case is still open, we are following up new lines of inquiry all the time and we are confident that we will eventually make an arrest.' She always reminded them that she understood their frustration and pain and there were four other families feeling that same frustration and pain, 'so you can be certain we're not going to let it go.' It wasn't much consolation for them. This was the only murder victim's family still in regular contact with her. All the others seemed to have given up, although Adele's brother would sometimes send Nina a three word email. "Any new news?'

Jules thought it was time for another zoom meeting with all the police who had been involved in the murders since the beginning. Some had moved on or been taken off the case to address current issues. One or two had just let things slide - deciding it was all too hard and they'd have to wait for the killer to make a mistake. But for Jack, Nina, Constable Jackson

- even DS Crossley, who had all been first on the scene when the bodies were discovered, the horror of the murders was burnt into their memory. They were as determined as ever to catch the bastard.

Jules had put together a brief presentation about each victim in terms of what we knew and what we suspected.

She started with Lily Fernandez because 'she's clearly the first victim - or the first one we know about anyway. So what do we know?"

Jules clicked onto the one photo they had of Lily, paused a second to let them all put a face to the skeleton, before flicking up the points she was making, one by one.

1. Lily had overstayed her visa and was on the run from immigration.
2. She had been living in Manoora for almost 5 months working as a sex worker in an unofficial brothel.
3. Liked by the women there.
4. No run-ins with any locals.
5. Very religious and attended mass when the priest came to town.
6. Was pregnant according to Bojan Katic and more or less confirmed by Father Mulcahy who claimed she was 'conflicted.' Bojan denied being the father but probably was. However if she tried the 'marry me' threat to someone else who could possibly have been the father, that might be a motive. I would put this low on the list however, because if the 'father of the baby' was the murderer and he was just trying to get rid of her, it was highly unlikely he was involved in any of the other murders.
7. Her death was almost definitely caused by a heavy blow to the left hand side of her face, severe enough to crush her

skull and shatter her jaw, but no weapon was found in the vicinity of the body.

8. After speaking to Cheryl Hinkler, we have ascertained that she had been missing 5 years and 7 months when her remains were found.

9. No serious effort had been made to bury her, but it appeared she had been wrapped in a sheet of clear plastic of the type available from any large hardware store, then placed in a naturally occurring shallow grave.

Jules flicked back to the photo.

'It is pretty amazing that in all that time no one found her - but dingo's obviously did. The plastic had been ripped around one end and both feet, plus one forearm and hand were missing - clearly ripped off rather than cut. There were also a number of other parts of her skeleton that showed signs of having been bitten by wild dogs.

The question I have about Lily is this: Did she decide she had no choice but to terminate the pregnancy and if so who did she ask for help? I've been thinking about this a lot and I feel certain that this is the key to what happened to Lily. Maybe whoever helped her botched the job and she bled out, so they wrapped her in plastic and dropped her in a remote area. Maybe the injury was added post mortem to disguise the real cause of death. And maybe in that case, the killer is a woman. Could explain why none of them are buried. If it's a woman, she might not have the strength to dig a hole big enough.'

There was a general feeling of shock and awe amongst the zoom crowd.

'The other question I have is - how could she lay there all that time - more or less exposed to the elements and no one saw her. There are rangers out there, prospectors, numerous mining opportunists - even some thieves dumping a stolen car - yet no one saw her for over 5 years. Doesn't seem right to me.'

Yes, well this was a question that had worried everyone. Especially Constable Nina Ford. But there had been floods through a couple of years ago and the body was in a sort of ditch which might have been filled with dirt once. Or the floods might have moved it from somewhere else. Even then, Constable Gardener only found it because he was investigating the car - and had seen plastic flapping around. If it hadn't been a windy day, the skeleton might still be out there.

Constable Gardener had many conversations about that day with Nina Forde and basically the only reason he investigated the plastic blowing in the wind is that he thought it could have been connected to the stolen car - that - and he didn't want to leave it out there to litter the area. That day had made a big impact on him too. It inspired him to move to Townsville and enroll to study science with a view to taking up forensics.

Jules Banyenan was ready to move on.

'OK second case. Adele Farmer. On her way to visit her dying grandfather in Mt Isa, but for reasons unknown, she leaves the highway and travels to Richmond. Last definitive sighting was in Broken Hill where she stops to fill up with petrol here, (she flashes up a still from the security camera at the petrol station)...although we have a reliable sighting much later that same day when a woman - since identified as Adele Farmer, was seen vomiting outside of the Richmond Post Office and tells the witness who offered to help that she has a migraine and will go and sleep it off.

She then disappears from the face of the earth until Joe Palmer, who has driven the backroads from Innisfail on his way to Hughenden before heading to Cloncurry for work, finds her body carefully laid out near the edge of the road. It was clearly inviting some speeding idiot to run over her and make identification and cause of death even harder. Fortunately, Joe is not a speeding idiot and sensibly didn't touch the body but instead called the police as soon as his phone was in range.

As it happened, we were lucky to have access to a highly regarded medical pathologist - Professor Peter Castleton and he was able to inform us that her death probably occurred between 6.30 and 7.30pm that same night and she'd probably been on the road no longer than an hour or so.

As expected, the autopsy revealed blunt force trauma of an extreme nature to the left side of her head was the cause of death and the attack had taken place elsewhere. When her body had been placed on the road, the blood was mostly congealed and so we know that some time had passed between her death and when she was placed there. Rigour was well established, which is why the pose was so awkward. (She points to the unnatural position of the hands and hips)

It was highly likely she'd taken a drug called Sumatriptan which under some circumstances can lead to serotonin syndrome which is apparently pretty nasty. However this is not a drug that shows up in the blood, so we don't know if she was ill with this syndrome - or still suffering the effects of a migraine - or something else entirely. But it might explain why there were no defensive wounds anywhere on her body.

She was also driving a hire car which has never been found, despite helicopters searching the surrounding area. So whoever bought her there probably did so in her car, then drove back to wherever they came from and dumped the car somewhere that we'd never think of looking.'

There was a bit of mumbling about whether or not the killer dumped her car first and took her body to the road in their own car. But that was shut down by Constable Forde who asked them, 'why would you risk leaving evidence in your own car.'

Jules took back control of the meeting.

"OK I have six questions here.

1. Where was Adele in the hours between when she threw up outside the post office and when she died?
2. Where was Adele killed, and kept for at least 3 hours before she was placed on the road? Was she killed in her car like Sarah Newhouse? Of course some of that missing time would have been taken up with getting her from Richmond to Hughenden.
3. Why pose her in the hope that someone would run over her? And pull her pants down to mislead us that she'd been sexually assaulted.
4. Why were there no defensive wounds?
5. Where is the car? Where are her shoes?
6. What was Adele doing in Richmond in the first place, when she was headed to Mt Isa?'

Nina Forde was now smiling. She liked that this was all going somewhere - even though no one knew where yet.

Jules clicked over to the next victim.

"Victim number three - as far as we know. Amy Moreno, reported missing after she failed to arrive to start a new job as a beauty therapist in Cloncurry. A job she was definitely looking forward to.

She had been traveling along the Flinders Highway from the coast, in the opposite direction to Adele. She'd stopped at the coast for two nights, catching up with friends and was happy and in good health when they last saw her.

No one along the route remembered seeing her - which is odd because she was a pretty glamorous woman and would have stood out. I suspect someone in one of the cafes along the route is telling porkies because he doesn't want to get involved. But what can you do? Anyway her car was seen along the way by a couple of witnesses - including a truckie who was highly critical of her driving, so we know she was at least on the highway, headed in the right direction.

She was found almost 4 days after she was reported missing but time of death was estimated to be at least 3 days before she was found. Death was severe blunt force trauma to the left side of her face causing massive injuries to her skull and jaw - almost exactly the same as both Lily and Adele - and the attack had been committed elsewhere - like Adele's - and probably Lily's too.

The body was carefully, almost lovingly - although I hate to use that word - placed on an old couch in an abandoned shack just out of town. The care in placing her body contrasted with the violence that had been perpetrated on her. Once again we have blunt force trauma to the left side of the face that crushed her head and jaw. But there was also a lesser injury to the back of her head, which may have knocked her unconscious without causing serious damage. At some stage she had been wrapped in something, probably heavy duty black plastic garbage bags, but the wrapping had been removed when she was left on the couch. Substantial residue of that type of plastic was present in her burnt out car.

Toxicology tests revealed nothing. No drugs. No alcohol. No health issues. There was some black substance under her nails but that has been confirmed as matching the material used to cover the steering wheel of her car….so I have 6 questions about Amy.

1. Where was she for the 20 hours or so she was missing until the estimated time of death?
2. Where was she for 3 days or so after her death before her body was left on the couch in the shack?
3. Why - just like Adele - were there no defensive wounds to such a vicious attack.
4. Where was she killed?
5. Where are her belongings? There was nothing in her car. And they weren't dumped at any of the charity shops in the region.
6. How did the killer leave the scene unnoticed? Although - we now suspect he wasn't unnoticed. And if that's the case, why didn't anyone on the ground at the time see him.

I'm not concerned about the burnt out car. That just tells me the killer knew it was filled with DNA, prints and other incriminating evidence and so fire was the quickest solution. It might not have even been planned. After all, we've never found Adele's car. It's possible it's burnt out somewhere of course, but I think he uses their car to take them somewhere or dump them and then he gets rid of it. Adele's car could be down an old mine shaft for all we know. '

The screen flicked over to a photo of Sarah with her family. Jules let her photo sink in, before she continued.

'OK now we come to Sarah Newhouse.

In the months prior to her death, Sarah had seen numerous doctors about severe menopausal symptoms and had even asked Professor Castleton if he could help.

On the day of her death she'd driven to Mt Isa telling her husband she was off to see a specialist. She was seen in two different pharmacies and twice at Professor Castletons rooms where she sought his opinion of herbal remedies for her symptoms. We have footage of her arriving and leaving. (She flicks up stills from the footage showing arrival and leaving times)

Late in the afternoon when Professor Castleton was out with Aunty Lydia looking for native lime trees - her car was seen parked in Professor Castletons car park but when he arrived back, it wasn't there. It hadn't been there when he left for Aunty Lydia's either. The witness to the car can't recall seeing anyone in the car at the time.

At 8pm that night, Ray Newhouse rang to report his wife was missing and not answering her phone. A quick check of the hospitals revealed there'd been no accidents requiring hospitalization of anyone, so the police did a run along the highway for a bit to see if she'd broken down somewhere. They found nothing - but as they did a U turn to head back, their headlights lit up something through some trees. Investigating, they found her SUV with Sarah strapped in the driver's seat. The left side of her face had been caved in with her son's cricket bat - but not while she was in the car. The amount of blood outside of the car and bruising to her arms and shoulders suggested she was pulled out of the car, beaten, then shoved back into the seat and strapped in. Her hands had also been placed on the steering wheel to suggest she had been driving.

Because this was the third victim in a short time, and Professor Castleton was at the very least a witness, her body was sent to Brisbane for an autopsy. A highly toxic anion - and don't ask me what that is because I don't know except that it's a poison - was found in her stomach, but nothing in her car or bag was found that could have contained the poison - interestingly, not even the tablets she had bought from the pharmacist that day. The pathology report stated that without medical help, the poison would probably have led to her death - if she hadn't been killed by the cricket bat first.

All of the witnesses and possible suspects were interviewed and cleared. Professor Castleton was out all afternoon with Aunty Lydia and staff were in his office at both times Sarah visited and saw her leave in good health. They were there when she would have returned and parked in the Professor's car spot too, but she didn't enter the premises at all - you can't get in without ringing a buzzer.

Her phone records showed that on the day she was murdered, she called her husband twice. Once to let him know she had arrived and once later in the afternoon when the call went to message and she just said 'I'll call you back. 'In neither call did she sound upset or frightened.

Earlier in the afternoon she had also called a friend in Mt Isa to say she wouldn't be able to make lunch with her as she was seeing a doctor and then needed to get home. Her friend said she seemed quite relaxed - excited even - at the prospect of having her health issues sorted out. They had agreed to meet next time she came to town.

Because her car had been seen later at Professor Castletons office, we did check out his whereabouts for the early evening. He claimed he was home - alone - and a dog walker saw lights on in his home at 7.00pm and thought she heard music too. So nothing points to him as a suspect.

Next came the obvious suspect - the husband. Both Ray Newhouse and his sons had airtight alibis with plenty of witnesses to back up their account of where they were. Plus his phone records showed he was in Cloncurry when he made the call that she was missing - and that was probably close to the time she was killed. He'd also made a number of other calls to her and to her friends a little earlier - from Cloncurry - asking if they knew where she was, before he called the police.'

Jules took a sip of water - 'So I have these 4 questions about Sarah's death.

1. Who was the specialist she was going to see for help? Everyone in Mt Isa denies having any appointments with her that day.
2. Where did she go the first time she left Dr Castletons? He told us he thought she was heading home.
3. Why did she come back and park her car there but not enter the building - or call him for that matter?
4. What happened after she left the second time? Did she have someone with her?

I probably should have added a 5th question there about the pills she'd bought. Why weren't they in the car?

There was a lot of risk taking in this murder. There's steady traffic on the highway there, so the killer was in constant danger of being seen. This is someone who understands the conditions, knows the country well and is very confident of their ability to get away.'

Jules took a deep breath before she went on. By now she had everyone's total attention. For most of the officers, it was the first time they had seen all the cases lined up like this. She took a sip of water and flicked over to the last photo.

"So now we come to what I hope is the last murder. It's been just over a year now, so I'm hopeful. But that in itself presents some questions which I'll get to in a minute.

Christine 'Chrissie' Gleeson. Foodie legend in the region. Well loved, or at least well respected by everyone she worked with. Owner and chef of a cafe that attracted diners from as far away as Brisbane for her special native foods banquets.

Killed late at night in the cafe kitchen probably by someone she let in and who she trusted enough to turn her back on. It's the first case where it's obvious that two weapons were involved and both were left at the scene. The first attack made by a blow to the back of her head with a meat cleaver might ultimately have killed her, but the killer wanted to make certain. As she turned to face him - or her - she was bludgeoned across the left side of her face with a kitchen fire extinguisher.

In this case, numerous cuts and heavy bruising on Chrissie's arms suggest she made an attempt to defend herself but I think the damage caused by the meat cleaver was too much. Why a fire extinguisher? Well it just happened to be within arms - right arms reach. He just grabbed the first heavy thing he could and whacked her with it.

Right from the beginning, this murder seemed more spur of the moment, more personal. In the other murders, Adele was placed, almost posed after being killed elsewhere. Amy too was killed elsewhere and posed. Sarah was placed back in her car after being killed - why? - and there were signs that even Lily had been laid to rest with her arms crossed. Chrissie was just left where she fell - contemptuously.

None of her regular diners were much help, although Gabriel the waitress was able to give us a good timeline and the possible sighting of a car arriving as she was leaving work.

The biggest clues in this case came from the Aunties that she regularly went out foraging with and who she relied on for recipes. They were all pretty close and they believe she saw someone at - or leaving - the shack the day Amy's body was found. Someone that she was reluctant to identify because their presence there was so unbelievable. Unfortunately the

Aunties weren't there with her that day - so all we have is 'perhaps' and 'maybe.'

However, due to the hard work of Senior Constable Nina Forde and Senior Sergeant Jack Harding, we have a bit of an idea that Chrissie was up near Fitzroy ridge which had a pretty good view of the old track that runs along behind the shack. She had her binoculars with her and the sound of the car going up in flames - well -she would have tried to see what was going on - and maybe she did.

In a way - this is our best shot. There's a likely scenario that goes like this. She's been thinking about what she saw for months. The more she thinks about it, the more certain she is about who she saw out there. Finally, after the death of Sarah Newhouse, she confronts this person. They come around to her place and try to explain it away or convince her she's wrong. Things get out of hand and he - or she - realizes that they've been caught out and decides the only way out is to silence her. She's whacked across the back of the head, but when that doesn't do the job, they have another go with the fire extinguisher. Interestingly, perhaps if they hadn't whacked her across the face, we might not have automatically linked her to the other deaths.

So I have only one question about Chrissie's death, but if we can answer it we have the killer.

Who was the person that Chrissie saw out there - who was so unexpected - maybe so respected or powerful, that she didn't come forward with his or her name at the time of the murder?

We still have a lot of prints from the murder scene that we haven't been able to match to anyone, so maybe if we can identify possible suspects we can start eliminating some of those prints.'

Jules turned off the powerpoint.

"Now that it's been over a year since the last murder, there's a chance that the killer, having gotten rid of the only known witness, has decided to stop. Or they could have died, or moved, or might just be going quiet for a while. Remember we had no victims between the deaths of Lily Fernandez and Adele Farmer.'

Nina butted in. 'No victims that we know of.'

Jules nodded.

'Yes, that we know of. ...but for now, let's work on the basis that he thinks he's cleaned up his mess and that's the end of it. I want each of you to come up with a list of people you think Chrstine Gleeson would find it hard to automatically dob in. Someone she couldn't bring herself to believe could be behind this spate of killings. Probably the death of Sarah Newhouse made her at last face up to the fact that this person was going to keep killing. It has to be someone who has lived in the region for at least 6 years - and yes, they might even be members of the police force. One of us. '

The others squirmed in their seats.

'She'd have to know them well enough to feel comfortable about finally confronting them and willing to let them into her cafe late at night. That means it's probably someone that she didn't fear. A friend or colleague perhaps. Maybe she was even hoping they had a good explanation for being out there that day. This doesn't mean we are taking our eyes off other possibilities, but it is a very promising scenario.'

Over the next few months Jules Banyenan's team interviewed all the possible suspects that needed an 'outsider' to investigate them. Senior Sergeant Jack Harding and Senior Constable Nina Forde had to be considered possibilities simply because they had been involved right from the beginning and were in an ideal situation to manipulate the evidence. Although only Jack had lived in the region long enough. 6 years ago, Nina was still in training in Brisbane. Just the same, their whereabouts had to be questioned. They were the first to be investigated and the first to be cleared.

Jack was not available on the day Adele's body was found. He and his wife had been at a family celebration out of town, but he was at the station with Turley Gardener for several hours before Amy's body was found.

Nina was on duty for Adele's murder and security footage showed she hadn't left the station until Joe called. She wasn't on duty when Amy's body was found but her housemate assured investigators that she was home.

Both had been called out the afternoon and evening Sarah Newhouse was murdered. Jack to a domestic violence dispute and Nina to what appeared to be an arson attack on some cattle station out buildings.

There was also the question of all the effort they had put into tracking down what - or who Christine Gleeson saw that led to her death. Why would either of them go to so much trouble if they were guilty? The theory was that they could have been trying to misdirect the investigation from the start, but the drawback to that conclusion was that both had alibis for the night of Christine's death. Jack and his wife and numerous other locals were at an anniversary party with the mayor and didn't leave for home until well after 1am. And Nina Forde was on duty that evening with Constable Turley Gardener. They spent what was a pretty uneventful shift catching up on paperwork. Constable Gardener, had taken the opportunity of a quiet shift to catch up on some study for his forensics course. Early in the evening, a local had come by to get some paperwork witnessed and about 9pm there was some loud shouting and banging on the doors but it was only bored kids and they soon left - no doubt to bang on the windows of some other poor buggers place. The phones were quiet too, until 12.10 am when they received a call from Jack Harding asking for a lift home. His car wouldn't start and 'it's too bloody late and too dark to do anything about it tonight.' His wife was wearing her best high heeled shoes and 5km was a bit far to walk. Nina had arrived at the dinner shortly after, taken the couple home and returned to the station a little after 12.45. Turley Gardener was making himself a toasted cheese sandwich and coffee. That only left their whereabouts for the case of Lily Fernandez. An easy one for Nina, she had only been stationed in Hughenden since her promotion 3 years ago. Before that she lived in Brisbane. Jack Harding's whereabouts were a bit murkier - although it would have been about the time he took several months off 'for health reasons.' All in all, it seemed highly unlikely that these two highly competent officers were involved at all. As for the police officers from Winton, Richmond, Cloncurry and Mt Isa - there had been a pretty high turnover of officers in the past 6 years. The only officer that came out badly was the junior on call at Winton at the time the initial missing persons report had been filed by Cheryl Tinkler and that was due to incompetence rather than anything suspicious.

Once the local police had been cleared of any involvement, it was time to consider other possibilities.

After speaking to Father Mulcahy again, it turned out that there was another, younger priest in the area who had never been interviewed. His name was Father Ignacio Gutterez and he ran an outreach center for addicted people out of a small church hall in Cloncurry. At the time he had a couple of run-ins with some of the tribal elders, mostly due to 'cultural insensitivity.' But the big red flag against his name suddenly appeared because for a time - until Father Mulcahy and the Bishop of the diocese stepped in - he was said to have been conducting exorcisms - or something very like them to rid people of their addictions. There were rumors at the time of 'unnatural' deaths, but none were able to be attributed directly to him. In fact all the so-called unnatural deaths were found by the coroner to be accidental overdoses, or organ failure due to long term alcoholism or drug abuse. But that didn't stop a number of people from suspecting his religious rites had something to do with them. As for timing, well, he had definitely been around when Lily Fernandez was living in Manoora and had been sent away for counseling and guidance not long after. He had returned to the area shortly before Adele Farmer's death and was assisting those priests who traveled to remote towns to hold services. When questioned, he had no idea where he was for any of the deaths except for Sarah Newhouse and Christine Gleeson. For Sarah Newhouse he claimed he was in his room - alone -meditating on the Second letter of Paul to the Corinthians. Hardly a watertight alibi. But for Christine Gleeson things looked decidedly better. That night he was in Longreach, having assisted in the baptism of a new baby earlier in the day. Father Paulson had carried out the actual baptism and assured the police that Father Gutterez was most definitely with him that night in Longreach. Father Gutterez went closer to the bottom of likely suspects, but was not dropped off entirely - the church had a habit of protecting its own.

The list of suspects to be investigated and cleared was pretty long. First on the list was Geoff Baxter the butcher. There's a bit of police wisdom that says the person who calls in the murder is often the person who did it and Geoff had plenty of opportunity in Chrissie's case. But he'd only taken over the butcher shop in Cloncurry 2 years ago. Before that he worked in Townsville. Geoff was only in his early 30's with a wife and three young kids - and between his family and his business he didn't have much spare time to go around killing women. Plus, there were just too many witnesses to the fact that he was in his shop all day, the day Sarah Newhouse was killed. What he did have however was a cool room and freezer where he could have stored bodies - but it wasn't enough to keep him on the list.

As more and more possible suspects were cleared, there were some interesting people that still remained.

Avery Jacks, a retired nursing sister who was known to provide all sorts of official - and unofficial medical help to women was one of them. She lived in Mt Isa but was known to travel widely to support women's health. For many older women, she was still the first port of call for any 'womens troubles' and was trusted implicitly. At first she refused to cooperate with the police at all, but when she realized that she really was considered a possible suspect she provided alibis of a sort that couldn't actually be proven.

'How am I supposed to remember where I was all those years ago?'

Years of standing on her feet all day when working as a nurse had left her with dodgy knees and for the past 2 years at least she'd relied on a walker to help her get around, so after an initial interview, they crossed her off the list.

Then there was Danny Banda, the chief ranger in the Corella Dam park area who knew all, and saw all, yet claimed never to have seen any of these women or their killer. Quite a few people had their suspicions about Danny from day one and he'd been interviewed twice. Once after Adele Palmer's death when someone reported him driving a silver Nissan XTrail that wasn't his. (It was his sisters. He was driving it for the day while his car was having the bearings in its front wheels replaced.) And the second time after Chrissie Gleeson was murdered because several people had overheard him having a loud argument with her over removing plants from the park. She had denied it was her and had taken him into her kitchen to show him the plants she had collected and explain where they came from. According to Danny, the argument had supposedly been patched up, but who knew for certain. He was certainly the only person they had questioned who had a bad word to say about Chrissie.

Danny had also grown up in the area and knew every track and hiding place. Every short cut. Every escape route. His ranger's uniform also gave him an air of authority. He was just the kind of man a woman in trouble might feel safe asking for help or directions. And he had no real proof of where he was for any of the killings. Partly because he was out on his own most of the time and partly because he just didn't keep track of these things. The suspicion in Cloncurry where he lived had not gone away over the years and so he was kept high on the list.

Also hanging around on the list but with no real commitment by anyone to take them seriously as suspects were Dr Sidowski and Professor Castleton, neither of whom were particularly well known to Christine Gleeson. (Dr Sidowski not at all except by sight).

But perhaps the most fascinating person of interest of all to appear out of nowhere, was Mt Isa Pharmacist Meera Shastri. Meera and Chrissie had known each other in Sydney - went to the same girls school and ended up studying at the same university in Canberra - although they pursued different interests. They'd kept in close contact throughout the years since, though not so close that Chrissie attended Meera's wedding.

Some years later, after she had escaped a difficult marriage, Meera sold her share of a very successful pharmacy in Neutral Bay, Sydney and bought a pharmacy in Mt Isa. Everyone said she was mad and would regret it but she loved the area and the people. She'd made such a success of the move, that in

the almost 9 years she had now lived in the region, her pharmacy had expanded to take over the shop next door and she'd
become very involved in promoting arts in the area, arranging
small classical concerts, sponsoring theatrical groups and promoting local tourism.

Pretty soon Chrissie started making regular visits to Mt Isa
to see her old friend Meera and before long, she too was sold
on the region and moved down the highway to Cloncurry to set
up her cafe - Cafe Clon. There was no doubt the two women
were close, regularly making trips out of town to explore the
region. How close? Of course people talked - two unmarried
women in their 40's spending so much time together. But then
to everyone's surprise, Meera abruptly married Sonny Chawla,
a solicitor and widower with two adult children who were both
away at university. Sonny had lived in the town for 25 years,
having initially run the legal department for the mining company. He said the landscape reminded him of the part of India
he came from and once he'd arrived, he never considered leaving. Unlike Meera, Sonny's interests were mostly sporting. He
was a major supporter of the local cricket club, often donat-
ing equipment and uniforms for those who couldn't afford to
supply their own - and a keen - though only middling, golfer.
But he was full of admiration for his wife who he believed was
'really putting back into the community.'

Chrissie seemed genuinely thrilled for Meera, and the marriage made no difference to their friendship. While Sonny pursued his sporting passions, Meera and Chrissie would be out
exploring the landscape and collecting native foods. Mostly -
according to Meera -' in the areas around Cloncurry, not up
here in Isa.'

So if Chrissie had any secrets, Meera would have been the
person she'd tell, surely. But when Chrissie was murdered,

Meera denied knowing anything about something she might have witnessed and Sonny seemed uncomfortably relieved that he had lost a competitor for his wife's time and friendship.

Because Meera had never come to anyone's attention at the time of Chrissie's murder, she hadn't been questioned back then. But now that she was, the details about where she was at the time of Chrissie's murder changed several times. She put her vagueness down to time. She just could not be certain where she was all that time ago - except that it would definitely have been in Mt Isa. Despite them being close friends, she claimed she had only found out about Chrissie's death after seeing the report on the news.

'Her death - and what happened was a shock - but I wasn't surprised no one had called me. She wouldn't have had me listed under my name in her phone because of a stalking issue from years ago - nothing to do with her death, but she just got into the habit of listing me under a pseudonym.' A quick recheck of all the numbers found on Chrissie's phone did in fact reveal that Meera's number was listed as belonging to Canberra Students Assoc.

After talking to Meera for a couple of hours, it seemed unlikely that she would have been involved in any of the deaths. The only reasons to keep her on the list as a person of interest was that she had lived in the area for the right amount of time and as a pharmacist, she would have been trusted by all the victims. But when Jules Banyenan found out that Meera also had an off-site lock-up that contained a refrigerated area, alarm bells rang. Within hours she had a search warrant and a team ready to search the place top to bottom.

The cool room was large enough to take several bodies, but when police arrived, all that was there were cardboard boxes filled with over the counter medications. That didn't stop the forensics team from meticulously going over the entire area in search of blood or human tissue. But there was nothing.

The main storage area was half filled with cartons of general non medical pharmacy products. Thongs, sunglasses, hats, baby products, that sort of thing. Once again there was no trace of human remains - or of any cleaners that could have been used to clean them up. Meera and her husband stayed well away while the search took place and expressed surprise - but understanding about why it needed to happen. But when Jules Banyenan took the opportunity to remind Meera 'that if you know anything, now would be a good time to talk,' Meera still claimed to know nothing. Jules didn't believe her, but she had nothing to use to pressure her.

10

Three years later, no one had still been arrested for any of the murders and the case had gone cold. The only 'positive' in all that time, was that there had been no more murders - or at least none that had been discovered.

The couple who had become the main suspects in Jules Banyenan's mind -Meera Shastri and Sonny Chawla - had continued their lives of quiet respectability. Apart from a 3 month trip they made to India for the marriage of Sonny's son, they had spent all that time in Mt Isa, doing what they had always done. Meera's pharmacy had grown to become the largest in Mt Isa - also offering a nutritionist and part time physiotherapist on staff, and Sonny's golf handicap had improved marginally. Neither showed any signs of guilt or anxiety and were not regarded with even a whiff of suspicion by the locals.

Amy's family had stopped sending emails and sunk into a kind of hopeless acceptance that they were never going to have closure. For the first 2 years, her parents at least made the trek up to Hughenden on the anniversary of her death and laid flowers at the scene. But the owner of the land had always been uncomfortable about the shack becoming a malevolent drawcard for tourists and shortly after the Moreno family's last visit, knocked it down. More recently Amy's dad had suffered a stroke and was confined to a wheelchair. He was losing hope that the killer would be brought to justice before he died.

Ray Newhouse, who had never been the same after his wife's death, had moved to Rockhampton to be closer to his sons - both of whom were now living there. He'd become a grandfather after his eldest son and his partner had given birth to a baby girl and called her Bella Sarah. In a recent conversation with Jules, he confessed to her that little Bella was really all that kept him going. 'I spend a lot of time building things for her. Currently I'm working on a dolls house. Keeps my mind occupied.'

Adele's father died of what the local paper insisted on calling 'a broken heart' but in truth he'd had a triple bypass a year before Adele had been murdered. The family, which had never really been close, had drifted further apart after her death and her brother Jason had moved to Tasmania to continue his Antarctic research project. Once or twice a year, he'd send Nina Forde an email asking how things were going. But even he had lost confidence in her.

Lily Fernandez's family had tried - and failed to get some sort of compensation as a result of Lily's murder. They did however manage to raise $30,000 on a Go Fund Me page, which paid for her funeral and then some. The police never did confirm if she was actually pregnant, and Father Mulcahy had since died without leaving anything in writing about his mobile ministry in Manoora. Or if he had, it had been quickly disposed of.

Christine Gleeson's cafe had opened and closed a number of times as an Indian restaurant, Thai take-away and gourmet hamburger shop. Each one had failed dismally as people didn't have the heart to eat there. Now the shop front sat forlornly empty except for when it was occasionally taken up as the local office by politicians standing for state or federal elections. In memory of her contribution to the region, the council had designed a native flower garden on some parkland by the river.

They'd added a large pergola there with coin operated barbecues at one end and tables and benches at the other. Its official name was **The Christine Gleeson Remembrance Garden,** but the locals had already dubbed it Cafe Clon.

Cheryl Tinkler, who had provided the police with their first breakthrough piece of information, gave up any hope of getting the rest of the reward and instead tried to make money by selling her story to the media. In the last 18 months, her rough life had finally caught up with her and she had been moved to a nursing home when it was clear she could no longer look after herself. But she was still telling her story to whomever would listen.

Most of the original police team had undergone change too. Jack Harding was now just a couple of months away from retiring. Nina Forde's good work had led to a promotion to sergeant and a move to Mt Isa Police. Turley Gardener had completed his forensic studies and become a police science officer stationed in Cairns. Meryl Jackson was on maternity leave and Marnie Chan was promoted from Senior Constable to Sergeant, working alongside Nina Forde. The rest of the local police who were initially involved had either retired, quit, or transferred to other stations. That meant that all the deep knowledge of the murders was now with Detective Inspector Jules Banyenan who still had high hopes of finding the killer.

There were two other key players in the case, still sitting on the sidelines.

The first was Dr Sidowski. Not long after the murder of Christine Gleeson, he had moved his practice and his family to Townsville for better educational opportunities for his kids - or so he said. But everyone knew that there was a small coterie of people who thought he was involved in at least some of the murders in some way - and while the police had never considered him a suspect for an instant, these noisy gossips did. Country doctors in small towns work long hours and his friends believe he just grew tired of the sideways glances of some people. He'd begun to feel that all the hard work he put into the community just wasn't worth it.

Finally there was Professor Peter Castleton who was by now close to 75, and still pottering around with his plants and overseeing business at his highly successful pathology lab. Even out here, Covid had led to a massive increase in the demand for pathology services. At the same time he had written his second book called '**Unlocking the power of native plants.**' It was currently being edited for publication and he was optimistic that it would be as well received as his first one. He was making less field trips these days, as his main guide, Aunty Lydia was too ill with kidney failure to move far from the dialysis equipment which was all that was keeping her alive. And anyway, he had pretty much documented all the known medicinal plants in the area.

✧

11

Jack Harding had been putting it off and putting it off, but finally his wife Ellen had insisted he visit the ophthalmologist in Mt Isa. He had cataracts in both eyes that had grown steadily worse, so that now he could no longer drive safely at night. He'd hoped to put things off until he retired, but Ellen had read an article somewhere about the negative impacts of delaying surgery and had gone ahead and booked him in. There had been a 3 week wait and she wasn't letting him get out of it this time.

To sweeten the deal for Jack, Ellen had booked them in for 4 nights at The Great Northern Hotel. The Great Northern had been recently refurbished back to its former glory - actually much better than its former glory - so it would be a nice change of scene for them both. They could have a couple of nights there to relax before the surgery and a couple of nights to recover after. There were also a number of good restaurants they wanted to try and the stage version of Rocky Horror was playing. It'd be a bit of fun.

Jack had probably been to Mt Isa 40 or 50 times since Sarah Newhouse' death and everytime he passed the spot where her car was found, he'd slow down to look. He didn't know what he expected to see there, but sometimes there were flowers left - less often these days. On this day his wife was driving so he could look longer, turning his head to look back once they'd driven past. Ellen knew that the murders hung heavily on him; they sometimes gave him nightmares.

'You know when you retire, you'll have more time to chase up some of those loose ends for your own peace of mind.'

"I'll have the time, but not the authority.'

'People might be more willing to talk once you're out of uniform.'

'I doubt it.'

Jack had never been beyond the reception area of The Great Northern. It had an excellent public bar with highly polished brass foot rails and a wide selection of beers on tap. But that was of no interest to him. Even in the days before he dealt with his demons, the hotel would have been too up-market for his liking. Filled with sober people having a quiet drink. He had preferred to drink with those who had forgotten what sober was. They were less judgemental.

Ellen noticed that the hotel had a spa and beauty salon listed as part of its offering and Jack thought she should indulge herself. She agreed. 'After you've seen the eye specialist, maybe tomorrow.'

Their room in the new wing was large and well lit. It would best be described as more contemporary than Edwardian, with the biggest bed Jack and Ellen had ever seen. The windows looked out onto a busy view of the town on one side and a small park on the other.

Even Jack had to admit that it felt good to be here. A change. A bit of luxury they hadn't experienced since their honeymoon years ago in Fiji. After an instant coffee and biscuits, courtesy of the in-room supplies, they left for the eye specialist's surgery. It was only about a half a kilometer away and a pleasant walk through town.

They arrived on time for their 1.30pm appointment, but as is often the case, were kept waiting for almost 45 minutes. Several times Jack lost patience and wanted to leave, but Ellen kept a tight grip on him. At 2.17p.m. a smiley faced nurse appeared, apologized for the wait and ushered them into an examination room. She would carry out some initial tests before Jack saw Dr Franzini.

The nurse sucked in a big breath between her teeth when she saw how little he could see clearly through his left eye and was only marginally more reassured by what he could read with his right. Another 30 minutes of various tests to check the health of his macular, and he was finally in with the doctor. Ellen had asked to join him for this part, fearful that Jack might underplay the seriousness of his situation. Dr Franzini struck just the right note between pessimism and optimism as he looked at the notes the nurse had passed on to him. "Obviously your left eye needs to be attended to quite urgently - both really. But let's do one, let it settle and do the other - say a month later.' Ellen listened carefully to what was involved in the operation and what to expect after. Jack only picked up, 'straightforward'......'simple' ... and then - 'I'll get the nurse to book you in - but Monday or Tuesday will be fine.'

So it was settled. Monday morning, 9.30am. And for the other eye, 4 weeks later on a Friday at 3pm. That would mean another night in The Great Western. Back at the hotel, Ellen decided to reward herself for managing to finally get Jack's eyes sorted.

'I think I'll go and have a pedicure. They say they can fit me in now if I come straight down. - will you be OK with that?'

'Sure - while you're there I'll go for a walk and look for somewhere nice for dinner tonight.'

The reception area was noticeably busier now than when they arrived. More guests were arriving and the bar seemed a lot busier too. Jack was just about to leave when he saw a familiar face. It was Joe Palmer and he seemed to be on his own. As Joe spotted Jack, he waved him over. Jack reached out his hand.

'Joe - what a surprise to see you here.'

'Surprised to see you too. You're a long way from Hughenden.'

'You're even further away from - where was it - Bermagui?'

'Good memory.'

'I thought you left years ago once your contract was up.'

'Nah - I've been back a few times since.'

'Thought you hated the weather up here.'

'I do - but I met a good woman and she convinced me I could get used to it. '

'So where are you working now?'

'Mine building maintenance. You still a cop?'

'Only just - retire in a couple of months - up here to see the eye specialist. I have cataracts. Bloody blind as a bat in my left eye.

Jack ordered a drink - soda with a touch of bitters.

"Staying on the wagon then?'

'Damn right, not going back to that place in time.'

'Good for you....I see that you never found the bloke.'

'Yeah - well - there are a lot of suspects....but…'

'Do you reckon you know who did it?'

'Not a clue.'

There was an awkward silence for a bit. Joe tapped his fingers on the bar.

'Maybe it's a murder stone.'

'Murder stone ? What's that? Blackfella business?'

'Japanese business. The murder stone was written about in an ancient story - well travelog really - by this Japanese poet fella - Basho. - He was famous for writing hundreds of these poems called Haiku - but he also liked to travel around ancient Japan to pay his respects to revered nature sites. A special pine tree, a view from a mountain, cloud formations over a bay - that sort of thing.'

Jack nodded along.

'So there was a bit of blackfella in him.'

'Yeah maybe - anyway he wrote a story called *'The narrow road to the deep north.'* It's like a diary of his travels. One day he hears about this stone - a stone that kills everything that comes near it. It sits on top of a beautiful spring some- where in the wilderness. It just looks like a harmless stone, sitting on a pool of water, but it's bathed in poisonous gas- ses from the hot spring. Probably carbon dioxide. Anyway the birds and insects and butterflies don't see or smell the danger. They just see a stone, conveniently close to food and water. As they are drawn in, they are overwhelmed by the poison and die. According to Basho, when he went there, there were so many dead bodies of birds and insects and probably small animals all around the base of the stone, that you couldn't see the color of the earth. And yet the birds and animals continued to come and die, not sensing the danger.'

'Is that a true story.'

'Yep. 100%'

'You think we have one of those here?'

'No mate, Not a poisonous spring. I think ours is a human stone. Someone who draws people in like he's a harmless stone - and then they die.'

Jack squinted his eyes.

'You're a strange man Joe…. but it was good to see you. Maybe we can catch up again after I retire and you can tell me more about these stone things.'

He put his empty glass down on the bar. 'Now, I'm supposed to be booking a place to eat tonight. Can you recommend somewhere?'

'The dining room here is pretty good - or try the Pukka Indian around the corner.'

The more Jack thought about the Murder Stone idea, the more Joe seemed to make sense. Jules Banyenan had long believed that the murderer was someone who appeared benign, helpful even. And they had all been baffled by the lack of defensive wounds on at least three of the victims. Like they'd walked straight into their death without any sense of danger. Even Chrissie. But should he tell Jules about the Murder Stone story? 'Nah', she'd think he had totally lost it.

Jack couldn't believe how well he could see out of his left eye since he'd had the surgery. "The colours are so bright - it's just amazing. Should have done it years ago.' So he was pretty keen to get back and get the other one done. For the last two weeks he'd been mulling over possible 'stone' people and had a chat to Nina Forde - without mentioning the story - just the idea that the killer would seem harmless, probably even helpful to the victims. They arranged to get together for lunch two days after his eye op and discuss a few options.

A month later, Jack and Ellen were just returning back to the hotel following his second surgery when there was Joe again.

'How's the eye?"

'Bloody terrific. This is the second one.'

Ellen took the hint. 'I'll see you upstairs Jack - but don't be long.'

The two men walked over to the bar.

'So Joe, is this your regular hang out?'

'No my partner Millie works here - head of housekeeping. I pick her up after work on Fridays and we have a meal in town here before heading home.'

"I've been thinking about what you said about that rock business.'

'Stone.'

'Right, yeah, stone. I'm meeting up with Nina Forde - do you remember her? - she's a sergeant now - works up here in Isa - anyway we're going to compare our list of suspects against possible stones.'

'Good luck with that.'

'Yeah well I'd better get upstairs or Ellen will worry. All the best.'

Jack was still wearing his eye patch when he caught up with Nina. She thought he looked like some sort of raggedy desert pirate. She made a feeble joke about him being Jack Harrrrding - pronouncing it in a crappy pirate voice. He congratulated her yet again on her promotion to sergeant and they headed into a meeting room at the end of the hall.

Promotion suited her and she seemed to have grown taller and more imposing. Despite the jokey demeanor Nina was all business. As they sat down at the standard issue desk, Nina opened her laptop and clicked onto a file she had called, **'The invisible man'** files.

'I should rename that. The murderer wasn't invisible. Chrissie saw him.'

Jack had brought his own file. He'd spent the past two weeks going through each murder, reading all the witness statements, and looking over the forensic reports. He'd taken pages of notes on each case and every possible suspect, right back to Joe. Every suspect was assigned a colour depending on which murder they related to. Black for Lily, red for Adele, green for Amy, orange for Sarah and purple for Chrissie. Any suspect that could not possibly have killed all 5 women because they were not living in the region at the time, or had airtight alibi's for one or more of the killings, had been dropped off the list.

His list still had the following names on it.

Meera Shastri

Sonny Chawla

(They could also have been in this together)

Danny Banda the Chief Ranger

Father Ignacio Gutterez

Professor Peter Castleton

-      And newly added - reluctantly - Joe Palmer.

None of the names surprised Nina except Joe's.

"Joe Palmer? How did he get back on there?"

'I thought he'd left the area years ago, but it turns out he's been here all along.'

'But was he here when Lily was killed?'

'Dunno. Never asked.'

'I don't think he was around here. - Besides he's not the type. He doesn't look - what's the word? - Benign?'

'Because he's a blackfella?'

'No it's because he looks tough - in a kind of Clint Eastward way. That's why I don't rate Banda either - even when he's wearing his ranger uniform. I reckon that if he caught you messing up that park, he'd really have a go at you. Probably try to kick you out, or find something to charge you with. You heard about that big public fight he had with Chrissie didn't you? Definitely not benign.'

I agree with the others though - and I've added one more. I don't think Avery Jacks is out of the woods. I know she's on a walker now -but does she really need it? And more importantly, did she need it a few years ago when all this happened. I mean she might not be as wonky on her legs as she makes out and she does drive a light coloured SUV like the one the waitress saw pulling up at Chrissie's.'

In the end they decided to draw up a circle. In the center, after taking everything into account, was Meera Shastri, Sonny Chawla, Father Gutterez and Professor Castleton - plus 'X.' 'X' represented a possible person that wasn't on their radar for some reason and probably had never been interviewed - a sort of Black Swan.

A little bit out from the center was Avery Jacks and on the edge of the circle, Danny Banda and Joe Palmer, although Nina still didn't believe they belonged there at all.

At the end of the meeting they both felt they had achieved something worthwhile - although that X in the middle was a real worry. Still Jack was sure he could put all this into a document that would impress Jules Banyenan that they hadn't given up. He would also spend the last weeks he had before retirement, honing in on Meera and Sonny. There had to be something there.

12

Jules used to tell her team that all the while new information is coming in, a case will never go cold. But the truth is, they all had more than enough serious crime to keep them occupied. Various forms of domestic violence resulted in a steady stream of victims that needed justice to be done. It was even worse when children were involved. Then there were the senseless stabbings and shootings and fights. No two murders were alike - and yet at the same time they were all the same. Jealousy, alcohol, drugs, money, sex, revenge. That's what all murders boiled down to. And yet the murders up around Hughenden way didn't seem to be motivated by any of those things. Unless Meera and Sonny were the killers. Then jealousy, sex and revenge could explain a lot.

They were all a bit nervous about putting the pressure on Meera. They didn't have the slightest bit of hard evidence that she was involved, just gut instinct. She'd only come to their attention at all after Chrissie's family in Sydney had asked how her best friend Meera was coping with the murder. There was the tenuous link that like Avery, Meera drove a light coloured SUV, and she did have a coolroom -but that was about it. But it was strange that despite their close friendship, she'd never once contacted the police - nor was she involved in the Hughenden memorial service for Chrissie.

So despite the suspicion building up around her, Jack decided to first have a chat with Danny Banda and get to the bottom of his run-in with Christine Newhouse, before Jules had another go at Meera. He'd called Danny in advance to explain that he wanted to show him some photos of people who might have been in the park at the same time as Chrissie. Danny didn't seem all that interested but he agreed to meet at his rangers office.

After a few formalities Jack took out his file of suspects. The first was a composite shot of Meera and Sonny. Danny moved to the window to get a good look at the photo.

'Nope. Never seen them here. '

Next he showed him a photo of Father Gutterez. 'Not in the park - but I've seen him hanging around. Priest bloke isn't he?.'

-Then Professor Castleton.

"Aw, that's that doctor guy. Professor or something isn't he? He used to come here a lot - years ago. He was always looking for something. You know - plant medicine, insects - that kind of stuff. Always did the right thing and asked for permission. Haven't seen him for a while though.'

Next a photo of Joe Palmer. 'Seen him in town. Never out here. It's not his country. His mob are from down south somewhere.'

And finally, a photo of Avery Jacks. 'Her - yeah nice lady. She's in thick with the Aunty's. They like her because she explains health stuff to them in words they understand. I think she helps them with government business too. Forms and that. Haven't seen her for a while though - but yeah - she's been here with the Aunties plenty of times.'

Jack thanked him for his help and was just about to walk away when Danny had his own question.

"What about that Chrissie woman? She was always around here somewhere. One day I was up there at the back of the park and this whole area which was full of yams had been dug up. Not pulled out tidy like - not just a few taken - but the whole area turned over like it had been dug up. I'd seen her up that way a couple of days before so I was pretty certain she'd done it.'

'You confronted her?'

'Yeah we got into a bit of an argy-bargy over it… but you guys know that already. Anyway, she reckoned she'd never do anything like that. Totally denied it. But if it wasn't her, who else then hey? Who else would go all the way up there? The tourists just stay by the lake. Anyway I couldn't prove it so I had to take her word. But you know what, since she died - there's been no more digging. That's all I have to say.'

'Could you take me up there one day to where the digging was ?'

'Sure.'

'Here's my card. I'll write my private mobile on the back. I'm out of the force in a couple of weeks. Still like to go up there for a look though. As soon as you have some time, give me a call.'

'You think it's important?'

'Might be Danny…might be.'

Jack climbed into his car, threw the file of photos down on the passenger seat and drove off. He'd just reached the main turnoff for Hughenden when a passing truck lost control of its load and slammed into him.

It took 2 hours to cut him out and another hour for the air ambulance to get him to Mt Isa. For a while, it was touch and go if he'd survive, or if they'd save his arm, or if he'd walk again. He also had a broken sternum, a collapsed lung and broken ribs. The truck driver got out of it with just cuts and bruises.

When the news of Jack's accident reached Jules Banyenan, it was like hearing of another murder. He was a good bloke and there was so much knowledge that he held, that the thought that he might not survive because of such a stupid accident was crushing. The police union assured her that he was getting the best of care, but she wanted to see him for herself.

When Ellen saw her arrive in the intensive care unit she was not pleased.

'He's still in an induced coma so there's no point in coming in.'

Jules ignored the anger in the comment.

'Are you getting all the support you need Ellen? Is there anything I can do?'

'Nothing. We can only wait. The doctors are optimistic that the spinal damage is not permanent despite all the breaks. Though who knows what he'll be like when he wakes up.'

'Do you know what he was doing out there?'

'That ranger Danny someone - he'd been to see him and show him some photos of people he thought might be suspects. Danny's the one who called for help and kept him alive until the paramedics and the fireys got here with their cutting equipment. You know it took them 2 hours to get him out. 2 hours! '

'Yes, we can all be grateful that he's still alive…. Did Danny see what happened?'

'No - he just heard it. But the police report says a truck was coming around the bend there and its load shifted and it just kept going - crashed sideways into Jack and then rolled onto the top of the car. I'm sure the police will show you the photos of the scene. I don't want to see them. (a pause and then) …just lucky that ranger was there and had some first aid training.'

'Well I'm going to be here for a few days, so if you think of anything you need, give me a call.' She handed Ellen her card.

Ellen looked down at the card. "Are you staying at The Great Northern?"

'Hell no. Police budgets don't run to that. I'm booked into a serviced apartment downtown. '

Jules checked in, made a list of things she'd need to get for breakfast and late dinners and opened her laptop. She scrolled down until she got to Danny Banda's number and called him. It went straight to his message service, so she left a text for him to call her. Then she called Meera Shastri.

Meera wasn't exactly excited to get the call and was more than a bit standoff-ish to Jules

"We've been through all this already. I've told you everything I know.'

But in the end she agreed to meet Jules in a neutral place - 'not here and not a police station.' Jules was prepared to meet anywhere, she just wanted answers, but was surprised when she arrived at the address to find it was a small amateur theater. Meera switched on the lights in the back stalls and they took a seat.

'Do you mind if I record this Meera - you're not being officially questioned. It's just a general chat?'

There was a long pause then she took a deep breath.

'Ok. But I might change my mind if it gets tricky.'

'Perfectly understandable.'

'Now Meera, the reason I wanted to talk to you again after all this time is that of all the people who knew Chrissie, you knew her best and yet you've offered us no help or insights into her murder. And honestly I can't help feeling that if she had seen someone or suspected someone of being involved in these murders she would have at least mentioned something to you.'

Meera shook her head in denial.

'No she didn't, I promise you. But I know you think I might have had something to do with it - that's why I was happy to fully cooperate with you searching my premises. I already knew for certain there was nothing to find, because I hadn't done anything.'

'But you were very close - spent a lot of time together.'

'I know what you're suggesting and It wasn't like that at all. We were just very good long term friends from school days, nothing more. She'd been very helpful to me at a time when I really needed it. ..... Ok- so I know she was suspicious of someone but she always said better I should keep out of it. She didn't give me the slightest hint.'

'You didn't have your own suspicions?'

'Me? Well I did think it must have been someone she respected, for it to bother her so much. She said she was just going to keep an eye on him. I told her - tell the police and let them keep an eye on him, but she wouldn't hear of it. Then after a while, she never mentioned it again. I did ask her once, what happened to the man she was keeping an eye on and she said she thought she must have been wrong and to forget that she ever mentioned it. That's it - we never spoke of it again.'

'This is a difficult question for me to ask Meera, but could it have been your husband.?'

'No...how dare you...no absolutely not. If it was Sonny she would have told me.'

'She wouldn't just keep an eye on him?"

'No - that's an outrageous suggestion - look you've got it all wrong - totally wrong. '

Meera put her face in her hands, then readjusted her position in her seat. Jules could see she was not happy about what she was to say next.

'Alright...I'll tell you the whole story, but I don't want you to record it.'

Jules reluctantly agreed.

'Chrissie.........she helped me escape from a very abusive marriage. He controlled my money, my friends - my whole life. I thought it was just a matter of time before he killed me. Chrissie was a volunteer at a domestic violence center and I'd known her since school. I went to her for help and she got me out of there at great risk to her too. It's not easy, you know. Why do you think I moved out here? I wanted to get as far away from him as possible. When the divorce came through he threatened me that he would turn up when I least expected. That I'd never escape him. We both thought that out here at least we'd see him coming. It was a massive change for her to move here too. At first I was nervous because she became very high profile but that's why she set up in Cloncurry and not here. And if you look at her website and social media, she was always careful not to include any photos of me. And that's also why she never listed me by name on her phone.

Jules interrupted. "Canberra Students Association.'

Is that what it was now? She changed it all the time. Anyway it took me years to trust any man again, but Sonny is very special. Honestly, he's not the man you are looking for. '

'So why didn't you tell the police this at the time?'

'I was going to but Sonny was concerned my name would end up in the papers - or worse my face would be on T.V. and my ex would then know where I was. I didn't have an actual name to give you or any information that might identify this person and he said the police are already looking in that direction. What can you say that will help? ......so....'

'Well keeping quiet all this time certainly hasn't helped. There may have been details we could have followed up at the time - or questioned you about. But it's too late now..'

Then she added, 'But OK I understand why you didn't come forward. We'll keep your name out of it - I give you my word.'

By now Meera was sobbing uncontrollably and there was nothing more to be gained by punishing her further, so Jules went back to her apartment and scrolled down the list again. For now, she'd leave Sonny Chawla off the urgent list. Time to have a serious talk to Father Ignacio Gutterez.

The good father made all kinds of excuses not to meet with Jules Banyenan. He'd have to get permission from the church, he'd been ill, he was about to go on a sabbatical - none of which Jules would accept.

'Look if you won't meet with me to talk, I'll issue you with a warrant for obstructing justice. '

He said he'd call back after speaking to his superiors.

An hour or so later he agreed to meet on condition that he could have another priest with him for support.

Jules made her way to a rather grand church property and was directed to some offices around the back. Father Gutterez greeted her at the door and introduced her to his support person, Bishop Bai Lin. It seemed a bit unusual to have a bishop sitting in on the interview - but as long as he didn't interfere with the questioning Jules didn't object.

'Now Father, it has been several years since the last death in this baffling case and we have evidence that suggests you have some knowledge about who might be involved.'

The Bishop interrupted. 'What evidence?'

Jules ignored him.

'You spent a great deal of time in the general area, carried out some highly inappropriate rituals..' She waited a moment for the Bishop to interrupt, but he didn't. ...and you were witnessed at one time going into Manoora and yelling and threatening the sex workers there with all sorts of biblical damnations. I believe you were asked to leave several times, and Father Mulcahy refused to take you along any more.'

'Yes, but I was in a bad place then. I realized I needed help and I went to Brisbane for counseling and treatment. I don't think like that anymore.'

The Bishop smiled his approval.

'Yes but while you were in Brisbane, there were no deaths here, then they started again only 9 months after you returned.'

'No, no, there were deaths - I'm sure they were deaths anyway.'

'Which deaths are we talking about?'

'Those two young girls- well I think you still have them as missing, but their families - and me - we know they're dead.'

'What makes you so certain they are dead?'

'I had a good relationship with some of the elders out there. One or two had asked for my help to remove some evil white man spirits. That's why I did the exorcisms in the first place. Anyway when I came back I went out there to apologize and explain that what I did was wrong. But they didn't think it was wrong - they just thought it hadn't worked.

They told me there were these two young girls - one was 17, the other 19. Both had gotten a bit involved with drugs and were doing bad things to get money. One day they just didn't come home. Their families went looking for them but nothing. They reported it to the police but they couldn't find them either. I think there might have been some kind of report put out in the local area - but no one saw them again. I tried to find out what had happened but no one will talk about them anymore. They think they have died - or been killed. That all happened when I wasn't here.'

'Do you think the elders will talk to me?"

'It's possible - but I don't think so. Look, since I've been back here I'm heavily supervised. I have to be- because I'm on medication that helps me to stay grounded and calm. I'm grateful for the support the church has given me and I wouldn't do anything to bring disgrace upon it.'

The Bishop clearly approved of this little speech but for Jules it was just hot air.

'Well if you don't mind, I'd just like to confirm your whereabouts for the two most recent murders. I understand that you were in Longreach when Christine Gleeson was killed, is that right?'

'Yes...at a baptism.'

'And for Sarah Newhouse you were...(she checked her notes) meditating on The Second Letter of Paul to the Corinthians?'

'Yes...*We have renounced disgraceful underhanded ways; we refuse to practise cunning or to tamper with God's word, but by the open statement of the truth we would commend ourselves to every man's conscience in the sight of God.*'

Jules looked up at the smiling face of Bishop Lim and added a few words to her notes. Then she thanked Father Gutterez and Bishop Lim for their time and reminded them that she might need to talk again. Neither were happy about it.

Then as an afterthought she asked - 'By the way, do you know Avery Jacks?'

'Is she that nurse woman?'

'Yes.'

He nodded his head.

"I hardly know her, but she caused me a lot of trouble. Once when I was out there to talk to the elders she grabbed me by the arm and told me to get out or she'd call the police. I tried to keep away from her after that. I believe she was the one who put in an official complaint about me to the church. .... She might be able to tell you more about the missing girls. The elders - especially the Aunties - they would talk to her.'

Before Jules rang Avery Jacks, she put in a request to all the nearby police stations to see if anyone had any record of the missing girls.

Nina Forde certainly remembered the case and Richmond Police confirmed that they had processed the missing persons report. Far from being ignored or swept under the carpet, there had been a large-scale search. Volunteers, rangers and police had combed the general area, right out to the farthest places the girls could have reached on foot - and especially all the places where they could have fallen, or been dumped in gullies and old mining shafts. People had been questioned, local news-papers had run the story but nothing had turned up. The girls were well-known around town - (the younger one often sang with a country band at one of the pubs) - but they hadn't been seen at all on the night they disappeared and it was thought at the time that maybe they had been picked up by a truckie headed for Mt Isa or back to the coast.

Nina also recalled that at the time there was some talk that there was a third girl missing, a white girl that they some-times hung out with, but no one else had been reported missing anywhere in the region. All in all, Nina felt that the appropriate amount of effort had been put into finding them considering how little they had to go on. 'Much more than happened for poor Lily.' And she agreed with Father Gutterez that they were more likely to be dead than to have run off owing to the fact that there were no reported sightings of them anywhere.

'There were drugs involved and that's never good. But we couldn't find a trace of them anywhere and there were no known dealers in the area at the time. Richmond, Cloncurry - they're hardly drug havens. So the stuff would have had to come in from Mt Isa, or from Brisbane.'

After quite a long conversation about Jack's accident and the likelihood of him making a complete recovery Nina brought up the topic of the murders. She knew Jules was in town and had spoken to Meera Shastri and Father Gutterez and guessed that Avery Jacks would be on the list too.

She decided to push her luck. "Can I ask you a favor? If you're going to talk to Avery Jacks about the murders, any chance I could come along? I was part of the original team that questioned her about them a few years back, and as far as I'm concerned, she's always been a suspect - or at least knows more than she's letting on. I'm keen to hear what she has to say now.'

'What do you think was her motive?'

'There was a rumor that she was growing dope on public land somewhere. If that's true, and these women stumbled on her while she was planting or harvesting, well......'

'Hardly a crime worth killing for...but ok. I was going to try to see Professor Castleton first but I believe he's in Townsville until the weekend - so sure, let's see what Avery has to say.'

As it turned out, Avery had a great deal to say. She ushered them into a sunroom at the back of her house and brought in a jug of water and some glasses while they made themselves as comfortable as they could on some old rattan chairs.

'I heard on the grapevine that you've been asking about those missing Pitta Pitta girls from years back. Is that why you're here?'

'Well actually we'd like to ask you some questions about the series of murders that took place around here. But we would also be very interested to hear what you know about the missing girls.'

'Fire away.'

Jules spoke while Nina took notes - Avery wouldn't agree to her answers being recorded, 'like some sort of damn criminal.'

'OK Avery, now I understand you've lived in the region for 30 odd years?'

'Thirty two.'

'And you used to visit Manoora regularly.'

'I wouldn't say that regularly. Every few months or so. They had a lot of girls come through there you know. I used to check up on them. Make sure they were using protection, give them advice - mostly how to get out of the game.'

'Did you ever run into Lily Fernandez?'

'I saw her there a few times, but she never really spoke to me about anything. I did hear on the bush telegraph that she was pregnant, is that right?'

'I'm sorry I can't confirm that - we have no proof either way.'

'If she was, I could have helped her you know.- so pity about that. Back then I knew a doctor she could have relied on. He'd do everything legally, properly, just wouldn't charge her or anything. Not that she was likely to have agreed. Strict catholic upbringing and all that. I do recall that one day I saw her crying her eyes out and I guessed there might have been a problem something like that. I tried to get Father Mulcahy to sort of give her permission to do something. I mean he wouldn't say go ahead and have an abortion. But he could say that God would forgive her and she wouldn't face the fires of hell because of the situation she found herself in. He was sympathetic you see - not like that monster Gutterez. '

She hunched up her shoulders and pulled a frightening face at the thought of him.

'A few weeks later when I saw the good father, he promised me that he'd told her that whatever she did, if she asked God's forgiveness and was truly repentant, God would forgive her. But I never saw her again. I did ask about her the next time I was over that way but one of the girls said she'd left town.

I just assumed she'd decided to keep the baby and had gone somewhere else to get away from the sex work. It was a shock to me when I heard her body - well skeleton - had been found. It's a tragedy really. Just another lost soul. Bloody religion.'

'What about the others?.

'The others ? You mean the missing girls?'

'No - we'll get to them later. I mean the other murder victims?'

"Well I've never seen either of the out of town women. What was the one who was found on the road?'

'Adele"

'...yes her - never saw her before her photo was in the local paper. And that other one - Amy somebody?...never knew her either. Weren't they just passing through Hughenden? I don't go there much. Cloncurry I used to visit fairly often but not Hughenden. - But I'm pretty sure I wasn't even around Cloncurry at the time of either of their murders..... Now Sarah - well I knew Sarah by sight - seen her around the supermarket when I was in Cloncurry. But I wouldn't say I knew her. Wouldn't have said more than half a dozen words to her the whole time she was here. I did have a bit to do with Ray though - he built this sunroom for me. I paid him - it wasn't a freebie for an old lady.'

'What about Christine Gleeson?'

Avery scrunched up her face for a moment then sucked in air between her teeth.

'You know, I think I might be the only person around here that didn't like her much. She really sucked up to a couple of the Aunties out in Pitta Pitta country. She got a lot of knowledge and advice from them. Made her name off it. What did they get? Nothing. - Oh yes - she would acknowledge them at the opening of her dinners and on her website and brochures. Did she offer any financial help or training? No. Imagine how good it would have been to take a couple of those kids and train them up in the kitchen. I know there were people out there that would have been great at that. But no. She held these wonderful 'all native ingredient' dinners and all the key people involved were white....... You see, that's what I hate about the way people just come in and make money off of them. They've done it with their art and now they're doing it with their bloody food for chissake. Well I didn't think she was a hero, she was a user. '

'Can you tell us anything about her death?'

'Not a thing. Look at me. My knees have been shot for years. Do you think I'd be capable of whacking her. She'd only have to give me a push and I'd be the one on the ground. Besides, didn't she get killed in the middle of the night? You think I'd go gallivanting around the countryside in the middle of the night on my own?

She looked over as Nina.

'I know you think I'm faking it missy, but I can show you the x-rays. I've put off having them done for years because I've got no-one out here to help me. But I'm finally going to get them done in a couple of months - even though it means spending time in a rehab hospital. Who knows, I might be there with that boss of yours - the one who got hit by the truck........ Is he going to live?

'We hope so - but he's got some serious injuries.'

'Yes, horrible thing to happen. Danny told me about it.'

Jules sat up. 'Oh you know Danny.'

'Yes, he's a good boy. Takes good care of his country and respects his elders. Now there's someone who would agree with me about Christine Gleeson, the so-called culinary legend. Once he complained to me that he thought she had been digging over some native foods areas up in the park without permission. I told him to report her to the police. I think he just spoke to her about it instead. Gave her a warning. She denied it of course. Who me? Never. Holier than thou some people.'

Nina looked up from her notes. 'Any truth to the rumor that you had been secretly cultivating marijuana?'

'Oh here we go - that again. Don't know what it would possibly have to do with these murders, but yes, I grew a few plants - just for my own use. Helps with the pain. Your boss knew about it, but I was doing no harm so they let me be. I certainly did not sell or give it to anyone else. '

Jules took a deep breath. 'Okey, so tell me, what do you know about these missing girls?'

'It's a sad business that. I used to go out there a lot - in an unofficial capacity - just to help the women with health issues, check their babies, help them with government forms, that sort of thing. Sometimes there'd be white blokes sniffing around. I'd piss them off. That professor guy would call in to ask about some plant or other - I didn't mind him because he wasn't making money off them - and then there was that Priest. Gutterez. He'd always be looking at the young girls - and I didn't like that at all. Aunty June told me that he was getting rid of some white man's evil but I was very suspicious about what was going on there. I told him one day to get out - leave the girls alone. But I know he still used to come back. If he saw me there he'd drive off. I spoke to Father Mulcahy about it and he told me to write a letter to the Bishop. The Bishop just sent a pro forma letter thanking me for my concern and assuring me that they would investigate the matter. Typical arse-covering by the church. After that I never saw him anymore. I was sure that when those two girls went missing he'd had something to do with it. But word was, he had been sent away for a bit of re-education, but I have my doubts.'

She paused to take a drink.

'But those girls couldn't have gone far on their own. They had no car - someone had to take them away. I'd tried to get them into a rehab program up here in Isa. They were both smart girls you know. I told their parents - they can stay with me. But you can't make them give it up unless they want to. I'd been up there just a couple of days before they disappeared and they looked ok. The elder one - Rachel - she told me that maybe she'd take me up on my offer if I could get her help someplace. I told her I'd get back to her....well who knows if she would have. But I definitely 100% believe someone took them - I don't think they had the motivation or the money to run off. '

Nina butted in.' What about the white girl?'

'Yes I heard about her, but I never saw a white girl with them, the elders never saw a white girl, nobody in town mentioned seeing them with a white girl.'

She shrugged her shoulders. 'It's possible that someone added the white girl to the mix to make sure the police took it seriously.'

'And do you think they took it seriously?'

'Yes - Surprisingly, I think they did. A lot of people were involved looking for them. The truckies that take the highway there were all questioned. There were a lot of searchers out looking. But there were no decent photos of the girls to hand out. That made it harder. There's only so much you can do without a witness or a body.'

'Do you think it's worth a chat with Aunty June?'

'Not a chance. You're talking about what are probably dead people. Chrissie and the girls. She's not going to talk about them at all. And honestly I don't believe she knows what happened.'

Avery struggled out of her chair. 'Is that all?'

'Yes - for now.'

'Well I wish I could help you more. I feel very uncomfortable about this- it's gone on for too many years. '

'Fortunately the deaths seem to have stopped.'

'Yes, well there's at least that I suppose.'

Nina climbed into her car. 'So I was wrong about Avery Jacks, but that priest...he's the ultimate in untrustworthiness isn't he?'

Jules paused by the door. 'Let's wait until we've spoken to Professor Castleton again. See what he knows about Father Gutterez. That might clarify a few things.'

The next day Jules rang the Professor to ask when they could see him. He was more interested in hearing about Jack's accident than making a time to meet but eventually she got him to agree that the following Monday would be a good time - although he wouldn't have a lot of time to spare because he was going to head out bush to collect some replacement plant species for his new book.

13

It was now a week after the accident and Jack was still in a coma in intensive care. But the signs were looking promising and the doctors were confident that if he kept improving at this rate, he would be woken and moved to a ward in a few days. But they also emphasized he would require a long period of rehabilitation - some in a hospital - but some at home too. They recommended that Jack and Ellen consider moving to Mt Isa to be close to the best facilities - 'just for a few months.' It was good news and bad news. Ellen had already moved out of the hotel and into a small, self catering place - now she'd just need to find a bigger one. She went outside to call their son in Ipswich. He was relieved to hear 'dads gonna make it' and promised to come down 'once he's out of intensive care. Don't worry mum, I'll help you.' On the way back in, the receptionist handed her a large manila envelope that had been left for her. It had a handwritten note on the back. *Hope he's going to be alright. This is his stuff that he left in the car. Sorry the file is a bit dirty. Give him my best wishes, Danny Banda.*

Inside the envelope was Jack's phone and wallet, plus a scuffed up, blood smeared file with some photos inside. Ellen was going to chuck the photos when it occurred to her they might be important. She put them back into the envelope, crossed out her name and scrawled **Attention Inspector Jules**

Banyenan. She'd drop it off at the police station close to her new temporary home.

The pile of emails and messages on Jules Banyenans phone all suggested that she should return to Brisbane as soon as possible, but she was determined this time to get a better handle on their list of suspects. She phoned her boss to suggest she stay until Jack was well enough to talk -'Maybe a few days more,' and that she would use that time to clear up some details with Professor Castleton and Father Gutterez. He wasn't that convinced that these interviews were going to uncover anything they didn't already know, but it wouldn't look good to drag her away from an injured colleague before she'd had time to speak to him.

'You're not thinking there's anything more to this accident than an accident are you?'

'No, no. It was an accident alright. The truck driver has already been booked for overloading his truck. I think that was the problem. The load shifted and that was it. Lucky they weren't both killed. But Jack was out there investigating the murders and I want to know whether he found out anything. '

'Okay - see you back here early next week. - Keep in touch.'

Jules took advantage of the weekend to drive down the Barkly Highway to the spot where Sarah's car had been found. Jack had been there just a few weeks ago and told her that the traffic was regular, but not always that busy. The killer had made an attempt to disguise the car behind a copse of scrubby trees well enough to actually commit the murder in fading daylight as long as he was careful. He would have had a good view of traffic coming from either direction -especially as at that time of the day, headlights would have started to appear. But two cars would have been harder to hide and the muddy conditions would have churned up the ground around the scene. At the time, there'd been no sign of that. The one piece of dashcam footage they had gotten hold of was completely useless because it was totally focussed on the road and the car's wipers were intermittently operating. No one else had come forward to say they had seen anything, even when they'd released photos of the car in the scrub.

Jules compared the photo of the crime scene to the place she was standing now. She was pretty close but nature had long overgrown any damage that had been done. She checked the mileage. 42 km from here to the center of town. Too far to walk, so there must have been another car somewhere. Perhaps he followed her out here. Or maybe they'd have to return to an earlier theory that the killer had an accomplice. Then she remembered that Nina had done some work on times and distances for Adele and Amy's murders. She sent her a text to ask her to bring any information she had with her on Monday - especially anything she had related to times or distances. Nina replied with a thumbs up emoji. Then she added a second message. Ellen Harding had left an envelope for her back at the station. It had originally been sent to Ellen and there was a message on the back from Danny Banda that said it contained stuff Jack had left in the car. It had been opened and re-closed, so some things had been removed. It felt like there was just paper inside it now. She'd bring that too.

Monday morning Jules and Nina met for a quick coffee and to discuss tactics before they headed off to see the Professor. He'd suggested mid morning would be best. Give him time to catch up on any urgent stuff that had been put on hold while he was away.

The envelope was a bit of a disappointment, but Jack had written on the back of each photo after showing them to Danny Banda.

On the back of Meera, Sonny, Joe and Father Gutterez's photos, he'd written. NO

On the back of Professors Castletons he'd written YES, but not for a long time.

On Avery Jacks, he'd written YES, considered a friend by the Aunties.

And on the back of Christine Gleeson's he'd written. HIGHLY SUSPECT.

That was a shock.

Was he suggesting that Chrissie was the murderer - and whoever killed her did it after she'd refused to give herself up to the police.? Now that would be a major turnaround in the case. After hearing what Avery Jacks had to say about her and seeing the note Jack had written on the back of her photo Jules thought it was at least possible. 'Except that she wasn't living in the district when Lily died. What the hell, this is all getting too crazy.'

Nina checked her notes. 'But she was visiting the region around then. Could explain the gap between the first killing and the others. And because she was a victim herself, we never checked her whereabouts for any of the other deaths. Maybe we've been thinking about this the wrong way all this time. I mean we thought she'd seen the killer. But if SHE was the killer, she could have been concerned about someone who saw HER. There was also the possibility that these deaths were somehow linked to Meera. Could it be Meera's ex who killed Chrissie?'

Jules grabbed at her hair in frustration.

"aaah....Have you got time to go through this scenario with me after we've spoken to the old Professor?'

'Sure.'

Jules put in a quick call to the hospital to find out if Jack was well enough to talk to them. He was awake - but still in intensive care and his doctor suggested they give him another 24 hours.

'I reckon he found something out there with Danny. The sooner we can speak to him, the better.'

Professor Castletons lab was only a short distance away, so they decided to walk. As they passed the Great Western Hotel, a woman called out after them.

"Excuse me, excuse me.'

It wasn't anyone they recognized but the woman appeared to know Nina.

'Aren't you that policewoman who was asking about those murders?'

'Yes..do I know you? '

'No - I'm Millie Abrahams - Joe Palmer's partner.'

'Oh yes. What can we do for you.'

'We heard that Jack Harding had a bad accident. Joe was very upset, but the hospital won't tell him anything - I was just wondering if you could tell me how he is?"

'He's in stable condition."

'So he's going to live then?'

'We hope so.'

'That's good to hear.'

'Look I'd like to stay and chat but we have an appointment with Professor Castleton and he's a busy man. I'll let Jack know Joe was asking after him.'

'Oh him....'

Jules, who'd been busily checking her phone, suddenly looked up.

'What do you mean by 'Oh him?'

'Nothing important. Don't worry about it.'

Millie turned and headed back up the stairs into the hotel.

Professor Castleton was his normal cheerful self. He'd had a particularly good meeting with his publishers, and had caught up with some old friends.

'Nice to chat to one's peers. That's the only thing I miss around here. The lack of intellectual stimulation.'

'Thanks for seeing us Professor. There's just a few gaps in our records for the deaths of these women and we're trying to fill them in. Dot the i's. That sort of thing.'

"I'll be glad to help, but I need to leave in 30 minutes or so.'

'That should be long enough. Now were you living in Mt Isa when Lily Fernandez was killed.?'

He searched his memory. 'Probably - but what's that got to do with me?'

'Probably nothing - but because you were one of the last people to see Sarah Newhouse alive, we need to establish where you were for the other deaths.'

'Goodness. Who would know - so long ago. But I was in Cloncurry meeting with one of the Health Clinics there when the first one was found on the highway.'

'Adele Farmer.'

'Yes poor girl. That's why I was called to the scene. When it's a bit complicated, better that it's me than a country doctor, even if they did have to wait while I flew in. That doctor, Sidowski - he'd done all the right things.'

'And where were you around the time Amy Moreno was killed?'

'Now that's a tricky one - because as I recall, she had been dead - around 3 days when she was found. Let me check my diary for that time.'

Professor Castleton scrolled through his laptop looking for hints about where he was.

"I can't be absolutely certain of course but that would have been just before the first lockdown. I would have been here, except for the few days when I flew into Julia Creek to train some of the nurses on how to manage the testing. I had a contract to process some of the remote testing stations you see. If you need actual times, I'm certain I can dig them up from somewhere.'

'Well Sarah we know about, but what about Christine Gleeson?'

'Hmm..well it was in the evening wasn't it? I'm pretty certain I would have been home. I'm a bit old to be driving 100's of kilometers at night.'

Nina interrupted him.

'You weren't quite as old then.'

'Quite right young lady. We were all a bit younger then.'

Jules got back to the serious questioning.

'Have you ever been to her cafe at all?'

'No, never. I was going to go to one of her bush food events once - you know - to see how imaginative she was, but I had another rather more important engagement on at the time. ...... I was actually quite interested in what she was doing. We both had the same aim really - to demonstrate to the wider community the importance of native plants. But no - never got there. Oh well, too late now.'

"Did you ever see her out in the scrub while you were out collecting samples?"

'Oh yes, quite a few times when I was in the Cloncurry area - often with that Indian woman friend of hers- but I don't think I ever saw her up here. She wasn't all sweetness and light you know. She had her enemies?'

'And who would they be?'

'I can't name names - I just heard that some people thought she was a bit 'overzealous' with her collecting techniques. Of course I'm not suggesting someone would kill her over it - just that she wasn't the goddess of food that some of the locals - and especially the tourist board - made her out to be. I had nothing against her though. She respected what I was doing and I respected what she was doing. On the odd occasion we even swapped plants.'

Nina had a thought. 'Do you have a helicopter license?'

'No - I may have many talents, but flying isn't one of them. Why do you ask?'

'Just curious at how you manage to get around such a wide area.'

'Well the police or emergency service fly me to various locations in their helicopter if necessary. Like they did for the Adele Palmer business. I did think about leasing my own helicopter so that I could travel further for my specimen collecting. But I enjoy the drive. It gives me time to think. And it would be a major expense for very little benefit. ... Now if you'll excuse me, I need to leave.'

'Do you mind if we walk down with you? I just have another couple of questions.'

'No problem at all - I'm parked around the back.'

'So why do you think Sarah drove back here and parked in your car park that afternoon?'

'I have no idea. '

As they exited the car park, they could see there was room for 2 cars, and that there was a door leading to a locked storage area on the other side. The Professor noticed Nina was staring at the locked door.

'The police had a good look around here when all this business with Sarah happened - including searching that shed. It's just where I store camping gear, a few tools, water cans, that sort of thing. You can have another look if you like. Especially if it's one of those "i's" you need to dot.'

'Good idea.'

The shed was pretty much filled with all the things Professor Castleton said they'd find there. A couple of camp stools, rubber boots, water cans, a roughly folded tarpaulin, shovel, camp stove and some cardboard boxes. One was filled with disposable gloves and personal protective equipment and the other with resealable plastic bags. In the front near the entrance was a folded up piece of equipment.

Professor Castleton took it out and loaded it into the back of his truck. "Other people have an electric car, I have an electric bike. I don't want to be cutting up the countryside all over the place. So when I'm collecting specimens I park my car on firm ground and take the bike. Folds up nicely, so it's very handy.'

Nina was impressed. 'How nifty is that - how far will it go on a single charge?'

'They say 80 - but I've never put it to the test. I mostly use it for small expeditions. 5-10 k's. I'm never much further than that from my car.'

'How fast does it go?'

'When it was new, I could get it up to 30 k's an hour. But I never push it that fast now.'

They said their goodbyes and left. As he drove away, the two women watched. Nina turned to Jules.

'Are you thinking what I'm thinking?'

'That bike would make a handy getaway vehicle?'

'Yep. He almost owned up to it. What was it he said? I use it so I don't churn up the ground?' We did find single tyre tracks at a couple of the sites.'

'And even though he said he doesn't ride it more than 5 to 10 k's - that thing will go much further. He could park his car quite a way from the murder scene and get back there easily....easily.

Nina looked back at the storage shed. She was now pretty fired up.

'And all that PPE and those disposable gloves - that could explain the lack of prints and DNA evidence.'

Jules tried to keep a lid on Nina's enthusiasm.

'Yeah but it's a really big stretch. All the things you're calling evidence - they're all essential to his work too. I think before we get too excited we have to talk to Jack to see what he has to say about Christine Gleeson. It's still possible that she's in the frame. But I will speak to the team about taking a cast of his bike's tyre tread for comparison. ...And we have to find some actual evidence that would tie him to the murders other than just a getaway vehicle. A motive would be a start.'

Nina checked through her notes.

'You know I don't think we ever took his fingerprints either. Never had a reason to. But now we do. We could get lucky and find there's a match somewhere. There's still plenty of unidentified prints from Chrissie's place and some from Sarah's car. Ooh this is looking positive - after all these years....and Christine Gleeson is back to being a victim. - At least for the time being.

Jules tapped Nina on the shoulder.

And you know what? I want to talk to that woman - Joe's partner..Mimi - no Millie."

Nina nodded.

"Yeah, what did she mean by 'oh him'...do you think?'

Jules contacted her senior back in Brisbane with the news that important new information had come to light which had the area's leading pathologist looking like a person of interest for the murders. He found it hard to believe but told her to run with it.

'Take another couple of days up there if you think you can clear this up. Wow a pathologist hey? If it's true we'll have to take a look at any other autopsies he's carried out on murder victims in recent times. Could open a big can of worms so you'll need to be absolutely certain on this. Be a big feather in your cap if you're right though - after all these years.'

Now it was time to organize the fingerprints. Jules knew there was no point in phoning him today, he was out collecting specimens, but maybe they could just turn up at his office in the morning and do it there. Would be interesting to see how he reacted. Maybe send Nina to observe while she went to see Jack.

The hotel wasn't that keen to let Millie have even a few minutes off to talk to the police even if this one was in plain clothes. Jules explained that Millie wasn't in any trouble, or suspected of being involved in anything illegal, but may have some important information that could help them with a serious crime. In the end they agreed to 10 minutes - any longer and Jules would have to come back when Millie finished work at 4.30.

Millie was equally surprised to see Jules, and gave a 'dunno what this is about' look to the manager.

They stepped outside and Jules explained that she just wanted to clear up something Millie had said. - The 'oh him' comment.

'It's just that he's a bit...weird.'

'How?'

'Lots of ways. Here's one example right. A couple of years ago my older cousin Jerry was diagnosed with pancreatic cancer. Pretty advanced by the time they discovered it, and there was nothing much they could do. Anyway, this Professor bloke came in to do some tests - take a biopsy or something - I dunno - when the nurse left the room, he told Jerry that he shouldn't let the doctors tell him there was nothing they could do because he had some bush medicine that could help. He said big companies overseas were working on a cure for a bunch of cancers using some of the plants he'd tested and he could put Jerry on his 'unofficial' trial. Well Jerry wouldn't have a bar of it. 'Why would I take bush medicine from a white man?' Anyway the nurse came back in and no more was said. But Jerry got his brother to ask some of the elders about what kind of bush medicine he was talking about and none of them knew anything about it - or about any trials. None of them ever took bush medicine for anything very serious unless they were pretty desperate. '

'Did he try to get anyone else you know of to try his medicine?'

'None that I know of, but other people from the mob started telling us strange stories about him too.'

'What kind of strange stories?'

'There was this one story about a couple of young boys - 15 or 16 years old, who said he paid them to catch wild pigs. $150 a pig - that's a lot of money for young kids - but they had to keep quiet about it. He had them pigs penned up inside a place somewhere north of here. I don't know how many but the boys said he was doing experiments on them. He'd wear these white overalls with a hood, a mask and rubber boots. They said he'd walk through this shallow stream of water - like a foot bath - to kill any germs on his shoes. The boys thought it was all pretty funny - like something out of a movie, but when the elders heard about it, they put a stop to it once and for all and told him they'd go to the police if he bothered the boys again. The professor said it was all above board - a legitimate study - but it didn't smell right - pardon the pun.'

'How is your cousin Jerry now?'

'.......what do you think? '

'Sorry to hear that.'

'The pig hunters are still around though. Let me know if you want to talk to them and I'll see if I can arrange it.'

'Thanks Millie - you have been incredibly helpful. '

Jules headed back to her unit to write up her notes. It had been a fantastic day. At last all of the years of enquiries and investigations had come together in one place, but there was still the problem of evidence. Weirdness is not a reason to charge someone. But there was a hint of a motive if you were caught running unauthorized medical experiments.

The Professor was not pleased to be asked for his finger-prints but he accepted Jules' assurance that they needed them for elimination purposes. After all, Sarah had been to see him on the day of her murder - and her car had been parked at the back of his building not long before her death, so they had to ensure his prints didn't match any on the car. He agreed he would rather visit the station than have police turn up at his business premises, ('It's not a good look when you are dealing with life or death matters.')

The results were sent to Brisbane to be compared against the numerous unidentified prints from all the murder sites.

There was one match.

Under the sink in the cafe's kitchen, they'd found a roll of paper towels. On the top of the roll, were some tiny specks of what turned out to be Chrissie's blood. Obviously someone with blood on their hands had ripped off a few sheets probably to clean themselves. These sheets had been found - screwed up on the floor next to Chrissie's body. But the smart thinking forensic team had dusted everything else under the sink just in case, and low and behold, it turned out the murderer had moved a bottle of drain cleaner - twice - judging by the ring marks on the shelf. The first was maybe when he had bloody hands and was smart enough to wipe it clean - leaving just one partial print. But then he had apparently moved the bottle back to where it was usually kept. This time he had left a few more partial prints. He'd also left one index fingerprint on the outside of the back door of the cafe. It was carelessness that the murderer hadn't shown before and maybe caused by the need to get out of there as quickly as possible.

When Jules was given the results, they came with a reminder from her senior to do everything absolutely by the book. It was such a small piece of evidence against a man with an outstanding reputation, and the skills to discredit the evidence.

The next day, Jules led a team to the Professor's pathology premises to charge him with the murder of Christine Gleeson and the suspected murder of Lily Fernandez, Adele Farmer, Amy Moreno and Sarah Newhouse. He seemed stunned, but after a few seconds, called out to his staff in the other room to 'lock up for me when you leave tonight. I have to go and help the Police and I'm not sure when I'll be back.' Then without another word, they left.

On the way back to the station, Jules phoned the hospital.

'I'd like you to give an important message to Mr Jack Harding as soon as he wakes up. 'Just tell him…we've got him.'

14

When they arrived at the station, the Professor still seemed unfazed by what had happened. He assured Jules that she would soon find this was all a terrible mistake - but that he would accept her apology for his arrest because he knew she was just doing her job. He did however want to have his solicitor present before he was interviewed because it was such a serious charge. He would settle for his local solicitor for now but would obviously like to bring in someone more experienced in these matters if it wasn't resolved quickly.

Barton Caddick was like most solicitors in remote towns, a jack of all trades. Mostly contracts and civil disputes with a bit of criminal law thrown in. But nothing quite this criminal. Still he was bright and keen to be part of such a major case. Until now, most of his work for the Professor had been tied up with his academic work.

After getting up to speed about the charges and having a brief conversation with the Professor, the interview began.

In the beginning, the Professor loudly proclaimed his innocence and insisted this was all a terrible mistake. But when it was put to him that they had found his fingerprints in Chrissie's kitchen and on the back door after he had denied having ever been there, the Professor froze momentarily then looked to his solicitor for advice. Barton Caddick suggested that in light of this information he needed to have a brief word in private with his client. In the interest of ensuring nothing - absolutely nothing, would derail the case, Jules was prepared to give the solicitor what he wanted.

An hour later, they were ushered back into the interview room. The Professor took a deep breath and closed his eyes. There was silence for a moment as he appeared to be thinking. Barton Craddock was just about to say something, when the Professor signaled him to stop. He opened his eyes, leaned forward in his seat and returned to his usual slightly condescending manner.

'Alright, yes I admit, I did accidentally cause the death of this Christine Gleeson woman, but as I will explain to you, it was self defense. But not those other women - absolutely not. They were all……. misadventures. I did not 'kill' any of them.'

It was hard to know who was more shocked, the police or his solicitor. Obviously Barton Caddick wasn't expecting a confession and he wanted to delay the interview yet again to consult with his client. But the Professor just wanted to get it over and done with so that he could organize his bail and get back to work.

Jules suggested that they should start with the Chrissie Gleeson case (for which they had actual evidence) and then move on to the misadventures. The professor agreed.

It was going to be a long interview, so before they got started, Jules arranged for water to be brought in. Barton Caddick also stepped outside to make a quick call - probably to a barrister in Brisbane and they all settled down for a long session of what they expected would be shocking revelations. Jules signaled to her team to begin recording.

The Professor took a sip of water and began.

'Obviously I'd seen her around, but I didn't really know her. We'd never said more than a few words to each other. But I did know that she was interested in native plants - like me - so I had some respect for her.

Then one day she phoned me out of the blue and mentioned she'd seen me on my bike, near the place where they had found that other girl - Amy. I told her in no uncertain terms - I don't know what you're talking about. I told her the only time I was anywhere near Amy was to do the autopsy. I said 'you're confusing me with someone else,' so she hung up. Of course I knew she may well have seen me that day - but I wasn't going to admit anything to her.

When she didn't call back I assumed she had changed her mind about seeing me. For months, I never heard a peep out of her. But then a month or so later when I was in Cloncurry on business, she came up to me again. She was pointing her finger at me and saying 'I know it was you. You were on that bike of yours. Who else around here has a bike like that ?- only you. I told her, if you think you saw me and you have proof - a photo or something - go to the police. But she couldn't you see - it would be her word against mine. And I think mine would have counted for more.

After that, she left me alone for a while and I thought that's the end of the matter. But then after Sarah Newhouse's death - well it all started again. Now she was suggesting that I had murdered all these women - not just the girl. Murdered! She wanted me to come forward and admit to it - every time she called she was more and more angry. In the end I blocked her calls. But then she started to leave messages on my office phone. I couldn't have that. I had to put a stop to it. So I drove down to just outside Cloncurry and waited until I knew the cafe would be closed, then rode my bike into town and parked around the back. I'd just planned to have a chat with her, nothing more. There was a waitress or someone like that just leaving. I gave her a few minutes to drive off, then I knocked on the back door and Christine let me in.

I told her we needed to clear this up once and for all because she could ruin my career with all these murder claims and nuisance calls. But would she listen? - No. She just went on and on about how at first she'd given me the benefit of the doubt, but when I didn't own up to being in the area she was sure I was involved - and now that Sarah had been killed after visiting me, she absolutely believed I was the killer.

It didn't matter what I said, she wouldn't shut up. In the end she said she'd give me until the morning to go to the police or she'd go herself. She said she didn't want to hear another word from me and I should leave. The hide of the woman! Threatening me. Then she just turned her back on me as if the conversation was over - just like that - and well - at that moment, I realized that everything I'd worked for all these years - was all under attack from this woman. Who did she think she was??

I couldn't take it any more. There was a meat cleaver there on the bench and I just picked it up and hit her. Then I realized what I'd done and I knew I shouldn't have lost my temper like that. I turned her over and she was still alive. I think I panicked a bit then. I knew she might live long enough to identify me and it would be all over. Then I had an idea. The best thing to do was make it look like the other deaths, so I found some of those disposable kitchen gloves and looked for something to hit her with. I could hear her groaning - I really just wanted to get away, but I knew I had to finish it. That's when I saw the fire extinguisher. After that I just quickly hurried around wiping down everything I could remember touching before I put the gloves on. I did have quite a bit of her blood on me, so I needed to get home quickly. I rode back to the car - still in a state of shock I might add - and put on some disposable coveralls I had in the back, so that none of her blood would end up in my car - then drove home. '

'What did you do with your bloody clothes?'

'Washed them of course. The disposable gloves and coveralls, I put in our hazmat disposal box at work. No one touches that stuff. And the shoes... I just threw them out with the next rubbish collection '

'And you are saying this is self defense?'

'Of course...it was her or me.'

'How were you in danger?'

'Not just me - my whole life was in danger - I mean my work is of major importance and she was going to destroy all that - destroy me..'

'But you weren't in any immediate physical danger. She didn't threaten you with a weapon...'

'She did threaten me....with the police....with the police. I was truly terrified for my life when I hit her. Terrified. '

Barton Caddock looked like a stunned mullet. He clearly could not believe what he was hearing. This time he insisted on talking.

'I really do think we should take a break now while I consult with my client. I am concerned about his state of mind.'

Jules agreed. It was after 8pm anyway and the Professor was clearly exhausted. They'd resume in the morning.

Jules went back to check her files. How had they missed all the calls between Chrissie and the Professor? Well actually it's not that they missed them but they only checked the last couple of days before her death and she hadn't called him at all during that time. Nor had he called her. But now Jules sent through instructions for her team to check Chrissies' phone records from the time Amy's body was found. The evidence was piling up.

Barton Craddock cornered Jules first thing the next morning.

'I've requested a delay in questioning for my client until after he has undergone an assessment by a psychologist. I contacted his wife last night - and although they haven't lived together for years, she believes there's clearly something amiss here. It's not normal behavior is it? We just need to be certain he is fit to plead. I've also arranged for a more experienced criminal lawyer to come up from Brisbane to take over the case. Much as I am confident in my abilities, this is going to be a big case and I haven't got the support staff or the time it's going to take to run it."

'Ok. I understand. What are you proposing?'

'The psychologist is a local woman - Isabel Henman - highly recommended - she'll be here by 10. I'm not certain how long she will need but let's assume at least a couple of hours. Martin Samios is the solicitor coming up from Brisbane. He should arrive about midday. I've sent him copies of the charges and notes from yesterday's interview, but he will need to talk to Professor Castleton too before we proceed.'

'So what you are saying, is that most of the day will be wasted.'

'Listen - you've waited years to get enough evidence to arrest him, what's another day? Much as I would advise against it, I think he's going to spill the beans. He's already confessed to one murder, it will be interesting to see on what basis he has judged the others to be misadventure - but you already know from what he has said, that he's involved. I'm sure you'd like this to go as smoothly as possible.'

At that moment a constable approached Jules and whispered something quietly to her.

'I believe Miss Henman has arrived. I'll arrange for her to talk to the Professor in an interview room - not his cell.'

90 minutes later Miss Henman advised Jules and the Professor's legal team that he was perfectly able to understand the charges, knew the difference between right and wrong and was mentally competent, so she could find no reason to delay the interview. As for any more serious personality disorder such as sociopathy, 'well, that would need to be assessed by a forensic psychiatrist.' She would write a brief summation of her opinion and send it through for the new solicitor.

Jules agreed to a 24 hour delay so that the new legal team would have nothing to appeal about. The professor was taken back to his holding cell to await the arrival of his new solicitor. He was annoyed about sitting around with a bunch of criminals, but once Barton had explained to him why he couldn't continue with the case - much as he wanted to - and that Martin Samios was one of Brisbane's most highly respected criminal lawyers, the Professor seemed to calm down and accept the situation. He didn't believe that whoever was his lawyer would make much difference to the outcome.

'I'm sure I'll receive some sort of punishment…I just have to hope that the court sees things from my point of view. They'll have to take into account my reputation and the fact that I have played a major role in the criminal justice system around here. It's not like I'm some sort of common criminal - for heaven's sake, I've actually helped them identify and catch murderers in the past. Do you know how many times I have been the consulting pathologist on cases before the courts here?'

At 2.30pm Martin Samios arrived, resplendent in sharp suit and with an equally well dressed female assistant introduced as Jennifer Chau. They were offered refreshments and led into a quiet meeting room where the Professor and Barton Craddick were waiting. As she opened the door for them, Jules expressed the opinion that she was keen to continue the interview as soon as possible and that the Professor had already been granted courtesies that perhaps another person may not have.

Despite the expertise and professional polish of his new legal team, Professor Castleton had already decided that to say nothing would ensure he was found guilty of the most despicable crimes and that he was determined to make his actions understood for what they were, rather than be branded as a serial killer.

Martin Samios re-read the psychological assessment and found no joy there either. He could only hope that the police had insufficient evidence to progress beyond this first murder, but from the brief conversation he'd had about each of the victims so far, it didn't look good. Maybe some sort of defense would 'appear' during the interview. He was already regretting taking the case and he was concerned that it would be hard to attract a top barrister if it went to court - although some silks would be attracted by the strangeness of the situation.

Finally he could delay the inevitable no longer. He opened the door and told the constable to advise Detective Inspector Banyenan that 'we're ready to continue.'

The Professor greeted Jules like an old friend, which in a way he was. Apart from looking a bit tired, he seemed remarkably sanguin. Martin Samios whispered some instructions to his assistant who quickly left, then unbuttoned his coat and sat down. The constable closed the door and they were alone.

After the legal niceties were out of the way, Jules began the interview.

'Professor. You claim that all the deaths - apart from Christine Gleeson - were misadventures.'

'That's right.'

'Would you mind expanding on that? Maybe by starting with the first death - Lily Fernandez?

'Oh yes, the Asian girl - I certainly didn't kill her."

Jules was taken aback by the denial, but continued.

'But you did dispose of her body..'

'Yes.'

'So you must have hit her - to cause all that damage to her skull.'

'Yes, but she was already dead. I just wanted to make it easy - in case someone found her - for the police to look at her and go - well that's how she died. Which of course you did.'

'So how did she die?"

'I really don't know - but my best guess is a catastrophic hemorrhage brought about by medical misadventure.'

'Professor, I'm not sure what you mean by that. Why don't you start at the beginning and tell us how you met Lily, what you know about her death and why you felt you needed to hit her so violently to create a misleading cause of death.'

He leaned back in his chair. His solicitor tried to intervene but Professor Castleton waved him away.

'It's such a long time ago, so I can't be certain I'm remembering all the details accurately. But let's see now.....around that time I had been hired to carry out some tests on a couple of miners who were accusing the company of dangerous work practices. I got to know Father Mulcahy quite well - we'd often have a meal together. He was the one who reluctantly introduced me to that girl when she approached us over dinner. He was her spiritual advisor, but not doing too good a job of it I think - she was very upset.

A little later, when I was out for a stroll, I saw her just sitting on the side of the road. Her eyes were all puffed up from crying. I told her I was a doctor and asked if there was anything I could do to help. Eventually she told me that she was pregnant - early days - but the father didn't want to know. It was the usual thing, she couldn't keep the baby but her religious beliefs wouldn't let her consider an abortion. Father Mulcahy had offered to find her a place to live in Mt Isa and then have the baby adopted out - which would have been the perfect solution - except that she was afraid that once she found her way into the legal system the immigration department would be onto her and she'd be deported.

Some of these girls....they have such tangled lives...... Anyway I asked her if she was certain she was pregnant – because other things can cause your periods to stop - but she'd done one of those instant tests and the result was positive. They can be wrong of course - but not usually.

It was at that point I thought I could really help this girl and help my work at the same time. I'd been doing quite a lot of work on abortifacients and emmenagogues you see - natural plants that can cause spontaneous abortions, and I hadn't been able to test my combinations on anyone. She'd be the perfect candidate.

So I told her those tests are not 100% accurate, but I had a natural formula that she could take, and if she wasn't pregnant but just had a hormonal issue that made her body think she was - well..it would fix it. She was a bit confused, but I told her she wouldn't be having an abortion - it would just give her body a chance to correct itself. And I explained to her that if she really was pregnant, it wouldn't have any effect on her, or her baby at all. It was a bit of a fib of course and I know I shouldn't have spun her a story like that, but you know how religion works. As long as you don't believe you're doing anything wrong, you don't feel guilty. I told her that if the medicine 'fixed her' she would be able to tell Father Mulcahy with an honest heart, that it was all a mistake and she wasn't pregnant after all.

But I didn't push it. I just gave her my number and said she should think about it and let me know if she wanted my help. I'd be back in town the next week and could bring the herbal medicine with me. I hadn't even left the town when she called to ask me to bring the medicine. Her main concern was how much I was going to charge her, but I promised I was happy to help free of charge. I did tell her it would take a couple of hours to begin working and so she would need somewhere comfortable and private to stay. She said she knew just the place and made me promise again that she would not be having an abortion. I'd already lied once - so in for a penny, in for a pound - I promised her it was all completely natural, no drugs. Which was true. It was all natural.

I must admit, I was quite excited about seeing how effective my extract would be. I packed several doses and also some plastic sheeting in case things got a bit bloody. I never thought for a minute there would be a serious problem, but there you go.

Anyway she had arranged to stay in the caravan of one of her clients who was away for a few days. It was walking distance from town, but out on its own. Inside was fairly cramped and not exactly hospital conditions, but I put the plastic down on the bed and made her comfortable. We had a little chat about what to expect and I mixed two doses. She drank one while I watched - and I told her to drink the next dose in 30 minutes. - I had to meet with the mine management over the results of the tests I had carried out and I told her I would come back as soon as possible. In the meantime she should just relax - there was nothing to worry about.

Jules butted in. 'How long were you away?'

"The meeting did go on a bit longer than I'd thought and they'd arranged a boardroom lunch, so it was just about 4 hours before I got back to the caravan. '

Jules noticed he was twisting his fingers nervously as he thought about what he was going to say next.

'Well, what a disappointment. There she was, covered in blood and I'm afraid, she was dead. Obviously the medication worked - she had hemorrhaged, but perhaps it was too strong - or she might just have had some sort of clotting disorder. I really wanted to conduct an autopsy to find out what had happened, but of course that was impossible beyond collecting some blood samples for testing.

So there I was with this deceased woman. I didn't know what to do next. I couldn't just leave her there. I checked around the place and saw that fortunately the client had left his car there and the keys were in the glove box. So I waited until it was just around dusk, wrapped her in the plastic, put her into the boot of the car and just drove further out into the bush. I had done some specimen collecting out there on one of my previous visits, so I knew a couple of places I could leave her, but I'd only been able to find a small shovel at the caravan so I couldn't dig a very deep hole. At the time I thought there was a good chance she'd be found pretty quickly, so I decided to create an obvious cause of death to avoid any confusion. I hit her hard across the face with the car jack, then covered her with the rest of the plastic and put her into a natural gully. Then I used the spade to do a bit of a crude burial with some dead branches and so on. After that, I drove back to the caravan, cleaned up the rest of the mess, put the car keys back into the glove box and walked back to town. I got back late - not sure of the time, but everything was closed and I couldn't get anything to eat. I had to go to bed hungry - not ideal. So as you can see, I didn't kill her. I don't even know for certain if the medicine had anything to do with it. The blood tests didn't end up revealing anything. Really the only thing I'm confessing to is improper handling of a dead body.'

Jules was angry now, but trying to keep in her emotions.

'So you think that giving a woman an untested experimental concoction and just leaving her there, played no part in her death?'

The Professor looked down at his hands again, which were now trembling slightly.

'In all probability it may have contributed to her death, but without a proper post mortem you only have the crushed skull. It was a worrying time for me too you know - I didn't know if she'd spoken to anyone about me - and although I was wearing gloves for most of the time, my DNA was bound to be on her body - and in the caravan. Certainly in the car. And I'd had to leave the jack out there in the bush because I had no way of cleaning it. I dumped it as far away from the body as I could but I was very relieved when they had some heavy rain a couple of days later. I thought that would probably fix the jack problem.'

Throughout the entire confession Martin Samios had been trying to interject, shut down and generally stop the Professor from incriminating himself but nothing worked. It was now 6pm and the interview had been emotionally draining for everyone involved. Jules felt sick to her stomach knowing there were another three to go. She called a halt for the day and advised Martin Samios that they would resume the next morning at 8.30am.

Samios wanted to follow Professor Castleton back to his cell to discuss the day's revelation, but the Professor wouldn't hear of it. He just wanted to eat and go to sleep. 'I think I have already established that I wasn't there when she died, so I couldn't have killed her.'

Martin Samios bailed Jules up in the corridor.

"He's right, you know DS Banyenan. He wasn't there when she died, and who knows who else was in that caravan with her. He was gone 4 hours or so - that's a lot of time for someone else to come along and kill her. I certainly haven't seen or heard anything today that proves conclusively he did it.'

15

Martin Samios was deep in conversation with his assistant when Jules arrived at the station. Neither looked very happy but they stopped talking the minute they saw Jules arrive. He approached her, 'I'm really worried about my client's mental state.'

'You'll have plenty of time to get a detailed psychiatric assessment before any trial. Meanwhile, we have a psychologist's report that says he understands the charges and is mentally competent - and that's certainly my experience of him - so we're going to continue to interview him about these deaths.'

They both entered the room where the Professor sat waiting. He looked less tired this morning and almost keen to get started.

Without so much as a 'good morning,' Jules began the questioning.

'Let's talk about Adele Farmer.'

'What do you want to know?'

'Everything. What say we start with how you came to meet up with her and go from there.'

'Yes, well as I recall, that was at the very beginning of the Covid outbreak. I'd driven down to Cloncurry to supervise a rather tricky autopsy. A man who had been shot and stabbed by two different people. They needed someone with my experience to work out which attacker was the murderer - or if in fact it was a combination of the two attacks....either way I.... '

Jules butted in. 'I'm not interested in that case.'

The Professor looked offended.

'Alright, alright. I'm just providing context. It helps me to remember. All this happened a long time ago and some of the events are a bit vague now. Where was I now? Oh yes, I decided to drive down because I had also been asked to train up some health workers in Richmond on how to use the Covid testing kits and I thought I might as well kill two birds with one stone so to speak. Do them both on the same trip.

I finished the autopsy just before lunch, drove to Richmond, demonstrated the testing kits and booked a room at the local motel to have a shower and freshen up. I'd planned on having something to eat and then head back to Cloncurry for the night. I had the room at the very end of the motel building and there's a big shady tree next to it. When I got back to my room, her car was parked right there in the shade under the tree, and I could see straight away that she wasn't well. The car door was open and she had flipped the driver's seat back so that she could lay back flat. I offered to help her and she told me she thought she was having a bad reaction to some migraine medication. I knew what she was talking about right away. I told her that I was - am - a specialist pathologist, that I could see what was happening. I explained that I could give her something that would relieve the symptoms but she'd have to sleep for a while.'

'Why didn't you just take her to the health clinic?'

'No need - I knew what I was doing. So I helped her into the motel room, made her comfortable, you know - took off her shoes - that sort of thing and gave her a tincture of some plant extracts that have a sedative effect. I went to the toilet and when I came back into the room she was struggling to breath. I suspected she was having an anaphylactic reaction to the medication. I don't carry around an epi pen, so there was nothing I could do but try to reassure her and keep her calm and wait to see if she got over it. '

'You could have sought medical help.'

'I am medical help. But if I took her somewhere else I'd have to explain what I'd given her - there would have been all sorts of complications. I was already worried that someone might have seen me take her into my room. Anyway, she didn't die straight away and I was hopeful she'd recover, but unfortunately…well that was that.'

'So what did you do next?'

'I knew I had to move her. I couldn't leave her in my room. … I did think about just putting her back in the car, closing the door and leaving her for someone else to find. But I knew my DNA would have been all over her clothes. Anyway there were a few too many people around. If I waited until night, rigor would have already set in and I'd never get her into the car properly. The first thing I needed to attend to was getting rid of my DNA and fingerprints on anything connected to her. Fortunately she had a whole suitcase of clothes in her car - so I put on some PPE I had with me - you know - for the Covid demonstrations - and changed her clothes, then I arranged her body in a way that it would fit into the boot of the car. Once it started to get dark and I couldn't see anyone around - I loaded her into the boot of her car and put my bike into the back seat and drove as quickly as I could to Hughenden.'

'Why Hughenden?'

'Because I wanted to leave her somewhere far away from where I was supposed to be. In hindsight, I would have been better off just driving into the bush somewhere and leaving her but I was very upset and not thinking straight.'

Martin Samios rubbed his temples furiously as if trying to make the pain of what he was hearing go away. There he was, stuck in a country town with a client that was confessing to the grossest acts without the slightest hint of remorse. He tried again to get Jules to stop the interview but she just shook her head. The show would go on.

'And what did you do then?'

'It was completely dark before I got to Hughenden, but there was too much traffic on the highway, so I decided to leave her on one of the back roads. I didn't have anything to use to bury her but I thought maybe leave her on the road where someone might run over her in the dark. Then I started to worry that maybe no one would come through until the morning and they'd see the body and not run over it - my mind was going all over the place. I needed to have an obvious cause of death. That's when I remembered how I disguised the other girl....'

Jules volunteered the name without even looking up at the Professor. 'Lily'

'Yes - Lily - Sure enough there was a jack in the boot so I hit her pretty hard across the face then laid her face down on the road. She'd already been dead for a few hours by then so there was very little blood.

Anyway I was about to leave when I remembered I hadn't put any panties on her - or shoes - but as I was putting on her panties, I saw car headlights in the distance, coming from the direction of Hughenden, so I just turned her face down and left her as she was. I didn't bother with the shoes.

Fortunately the car turned off somewhere, but it was a warning that I couldn't afford to hang around so I left.'

'What did you do with her car?'

'Well that was my next problem, I had to get back to my own car in Richmond - and then back to where I was supposed

to be - in Cloncurry. And here I was with a car filled with my
DNA, fingerprints, discarded PPE - all kinds of incriminating
evidence.

'Incriminating evidence - so you admit you killed her?'

'No - I didn't kill her - it was an allergic reaction. but I admit
I was there when she died.'

'An allergic reaction to something you gave her.'

'Well we don't know that for sure - but probably. But she did
take it voluntarily - I didn't force it on her.'

Jules buried her face in her hands. 'Then what happened?'

'I drove back towards Richmond, and just before I got
there, I headed into the bush as far off-road as I could get.
Then I set fire to the car and rode away on my bike. I was
hoping it would blow up and cause a bit of a distraction
which would give me free reign to leave town completely
unnoticed, but it didn't. I think the fire went out before it hit
the fuel tank. -Actually I was quite surprised no one found it,
it wasn't particularly well hidden. I guess no one thought to
look there. I went back a couple of years later and what was
left of it was still there. The fire hadn't done as much damage
as I'd hoped, but we'd had a lot of rain in the following year
and I was comfortable that whatever evidence there was that
might have led back to me would have been washed away - or
at least unusable.'

'What happened next?

'Well let's see. I rode back into Richmond, picked up my car
and drove to Cloncurry. I remember it was almost dawn before
I got back, so I'd been up all night. That's when you people
called asking for help at the murder scene. I was going to say
no because I was so tired, but I realized I would now have the
perfect opportunity to control the narrative.'

'The narrative?'

'Yes, I could manipulate the findings just enough to stay well clear of any suspicion. I couldn't lie or invent evidence of course, just place the emphasis where I wanted it to be. And of course I wouldn't go looking for things I didn't want to find.'

'Like the presence of unexplained substances.'

'That too.' He closed his eyes for a moment. 'Anyway, that's it. The rest you know. Look I know I'll face some kind of punishment for this - mishandling a corpse or whatever you call it - but I didn't murder her. It was just an accident.'

Jules gritted her teeth.

'Misadventure.'

The Professor smiled.

'Yes….misadventure.'

'I'll need more accurate information about where you dumped the car - just to back up your story.'

'I can point out the general area if you have a map.'

A constable delivered a laptop to Jules and she googled the area. Then she turned the screen around to face the Professor so that he could point to the location. After thinking about it a bit, and looking for recognizable landmarks, he settled on a small area.

'Somewhere around there I think. If you took me there, I could show you.'

'No thanks, we'll just keep you here for further questioning. I'm sure our team will find it if you're telling the truth.'

After a brief break, everyone returned to the interview room for the next revelation. The Professor was starting to show signs of nervousness - no doubt brought on by his legal team - and Jules was concerned he may have a change of heart and refuse to speak, so she was anxious to get moving.

"Now Professor, I'd like you to take us through the chain of events that led to the death of Amy Moreno. '

'Ah yes - well this is a case somewhat like that of that Lily Fernandez woman.'

'You mean she was pregnant?'

'No, no - of course not. I certainly wouldn't lie about something like that in the report. No - what I mean is, I wasn't actually there when she died.'

'So you are suggesting you had nothing to do with her death?'

'I may have,....she may have....maybe some sort of reaction to the medication she took.'

'That you gave her.'

'Possibly - but she was already quite unwell before she took the medication, so it may have had nothing to do with it.'

Martin Samios perked up noticeably. He could sense a possible defense. Jules however was confident that nothing he could say was going to get a jury to buy into his misadventure defense.

'Perhaps if you could start from the beginning......'

'Certainly Detective Inspector. Just for 'context' (he highlighted the word with his fingers to ensure Jules got his meaning) ...I needed to spend some time in the Hughenden area gathering specimens for some tests I was running. An old friend of mine from the University - John Summers - has a house just out of town off the main road there, just past that fish and chip place where the truckies pull in. Anyway he said I could use his house while he was out of town. He'd gone up to Rocky to visit his grandchildren for a couple of weeks.

On this particular day I'd taken my bike out and was exploring some areas off one of the fire tracks that run off the highway about 5 k's out of town. That's when I saw this woman trying to change a flat tyre.....'

'That would have been Amy I presume.'

'Yes…but she had no idea what she was doing - so - being a gentleman, I offered to help. There were suitcases all over the place where she'd emptied the car to get to the tool kit and spare tyre and she didn't look well at all. I asked her what she was doing off the road in such a small car and she told me she eaten something at one of the cafes that had given her gastro - from both ends apparently. Anyway, she'd driven off the road to give herself a little privacy while she relieved herself and cleaned up. She'd run into one of the potholes there and blown out her front tyre. So now here she was, stuck on a dirt track trying to loosen the bolts on the wheel with one hand while watching instructions on how to do it, on her phone, which kept cutting out because of the dodgy reception up there. At the same time, she was still retching.

I said to her, well..you're in luck. Because not only am I an experienced tyre changer and a gentleman, but I am a doctor too. So let's get this tyre fixed and I can take you back to my place and give you something for the gastro. Now at this point Senior Detective - I feel I should remind you that she was already sick - right. She thought it was gastro, but maybe not - and that's important.'

He looked smugly at Martin Samios who seemed to approve of that revelation at least, then took a deep breath and continued.

'So - tyre fixed, we put all her stuff back in the car and I rode ahead of her on my bike to John's place.

'You were on your bike.'

'Oh yes - there was no room for me and the bike in that little car of hers. Anyway it was only about 5 kms away but we had to stop a couple of times for her to lean out of the car and throw up again.

When we got back to John's, I told her I could offer her a pharmaceutical solution or a natural one. It was up to her

- I didn't force the medication on her at all. But she chose the natural one. I made tea from the herbs and suggested she could take them, have a shower to clean up and then take a nap until she felt well enough to continue, Meanwhile I would get back to collecting specimens and leave her alone. If she wanted to leave before I returned, I told her to lock the door behind her - I had a key with me. She was extremely grateful for my help. Effusive even. She said she was about to start work at a beauty place in Cloncurry and that I should drop by for a free facial and pedicure. Men have them too apparently. Anyway when I left, she was still alive.'

'How long were you gone?'

'All day - well all afternoon. - Got back just as it was getting dark. I was quite surprised to see her car still there. Disappointed actually, because it suggested to me that the compound hadn't been as effective as I had hoped.'

'So what happened next.'

'It was dark inside, so I thought she'd fallen asleep, but no... so I checked through the house and the bathroom door was locked. I called out, knocked, but no answer. The bathroom had a small window with louvers. I went around the side, removed the louvers and looked in. I couldn't see much, but I could see she was slumped on the floor, naked. So I climbed through the window, nearly breaking my neck as I fell into the bath. She was just laying there with no obvious signs of anything wrong. Like she'd sat down on the floor and gone to sleep. I checked her pulse, but it was too late. She was gone. Cold even.'

'I suppose there's no point in asking you why you didn't call the police?'

'No.'

'So what happened next?'

'I wasn't expecting John back for another week, so I knew I had plenty of time to fix the situation. The first thing I did was move her car into the shed at the back of the property. His place is pretty well shielded from the highway, but I knew that sooner or later someone would be looking for her and the last thing I needed was some busybody spotting her car. Then I suited up in PPE, dressed her and wrapped her in a couple of big black plastic garbage bags. But where to put her? Then I remembered John has a cool room out the back. He's a bit of a wine buff and he uses it to keep his wine at a constant temperature.- It's kept locked of course, but he'd given me a key to help myself 'in moderation.'

'You put her in your friend's wine fridge?'

'It's not a fridge. Just a cool room.'

Jules rolled her eyes at Martin Samios. He kept a straight face.'

'The next day I thought I'd drive around the area and look for a good place to leave her.'

'To dump her you mean?'

'No, to put her. That's when I saw the empty shack down where you found her. It was ideal. No one had lived there for years and the only graffiti looked years old. Plus - there was an old couch there. The rats had been at it, but it would make a good resting place.

Unfortunately, when I headed back to the house, council workers were out repairing the road along there. I thought it might be better if I wasn't seen arriving at John's place, so I drove on to Richmond to stay the night there. I waited around Richmond most of the day and got back to Hughenden early evening. By then the council workers had finished whatever they were repairing, so I knew I could safely move the body. I waited until it was dark, then moved her into her car. It was a bit tricky - it was one of those hatchback things and it was loaded with suitcases. I had to take them out to make room for her and my bike. I wasn't sure what I'd touched and what I hadn't touched in the suitcases so I had to get rid of them too, but they wouldn't fit back in the car. So I dug a hole at the back of John's property and buried the suitcases. That was quite a job, but fortunately John's not a gardener so I didn't have to bury them too deeply. Anyway, as you can imagine, by then, I was extremely tired and stressed, so I set my phone alarm for 4am and went to sleep. '

'I'm going to need John's address.'

'Of course.' He wrote it down.

Jules signaled to the camera that she wanted someone to check it out.

'So you woke up at 4am and then what?'

'I had a quick cup of tea and set off. This time I 'd thought to bring something with me to ensure the car would well and truly go up in flames. I'd found a bottle of kero in a shed out the back. When I got there - I couldn't see any other cars around - no lights anywhere, so I took her inside and put her on the couch. When I took the plastic bags off, I realized I needed to provide a cause of death, so I went and got the jack……you know, like the others. Then I put all the things - the jack, the plastic bags, disposable gloves - the lot - back into the car, and unloaded my bike. I was just about to splash the kero and set it alight, when suddenly there's a jogger heading my way. And not just any jogger, but that doctor - Sidowski. I quickly dashed inside and hoped he hadn't seen me. Not that he would have recognised me from where he was. I was already thinking that if he looked like he was going to come in, I'd set fire to the house first but fortunately he just looked over at the car and kept jogging up the hill. That's joggers for you. They just keep right on going.

Just to be certain, I waited until he was out of sight, then I poured the kero all through the car - and this time I took the lid off the fuel tank too. I threw some burning paper into the front seat of the car and whoosh, the fire started immediately. Once I saw the fire had taken, I grabbed my bike and headed off across country to one of the fire trails. That's where that Christine woman reckons she saw me. For heaven's sake, it was only about 6am at this point - who's out collecting plants at 6am? And what was she doing here? She lived in Cloncurry. How unlucky can you get!'

Jules found parts of his story inexplicable.

'Why didn't you just leave her in the car if you planned to set fire to it?'

The professor looked insulted.

'I'm not some cruel killer tormenting my victims. Her family deserved to have her body returned to them in one piece.'

Jules didn't even bother looking at him.

'So where were you when Dr Hui called you about doing the post mortem?'

'Back at John's house. I had a bit of cleaning up to do. Of course he thought I was in Mt Isa. He asked me to recommend someone but I told him you're in luck - I just happen to be in the area staying at a friend's house and so I volunteered. No one questioned me. Why should they?

It was strange to come back face to face - so to speak - with a body I had just left and to look at it dispassionately as though I was seeing it for the first time. From a purely professional point of view, I'd have to say I'd done a very good job of providing a very confusing scenario. Provided no one had seen me taking her back to the house, I was confident everything was under control. - Even the substance under her fingernails. I knew it was something to do with her car - but it was a nice bit of theatre.'

'Tell me Professor, when you did the autopsy on Amy, did you find a cause of death - other than the blunt force trauma that you falsely claimed was the cause of death?'

'I didn't look very hard...... but if I wasn't involved in the case at all......I might have said she was poisoned with something that affected her central nervous system. And of course I would have had to take a closer look at exactly what that was. But look, you're wasting your time thinking about it. It would be hard to prove I had something to do with it, because she was already unwell when I found her. She may really have been poisoned elsewhere. '

Martin Samios was making copious notes. Yes, yes, he could see a defense of sorts in all of this - or at least a way to muddy the waters enough to create doubt.

While everything was put on pause for a toilet break, two important pieces of news came through.

Richmond Police had located what appeared to be Adele Farmers hire car and roped off the area surrounding it while awaiting the arrival of a forensic team - not that they were expecting to find anything of any use. Between the fire and years exposed to the elements, it was barely recognisable.

And Hughenden Police had dug up the land in the back garden of John Summers place and found two large suit-cases. Both cases were the hard plastic variety capable of withstanding anything airport baggage handlers can throw at them, and still in good condition with only the metal hinges and locks rusted away, so the police were confident of finding some useful evidence. According to the report, 'Mr Summer was not very happy to learn that a death had taken place in his home, or that evidence had been buried on his property all this time.'

'Wait until he hears that a body was stored in his wine cool room,' Jules thought.

There was only one more case to talk about and Jules wanted to get it over and done with. Martin Samios agreed.

'There's so much to unpack here. The sooner I can get back to my office and sort it out the better.'

Jules passed on the information about the car and the luggage. He just nodded.

After a brief break, everyone headed back to the interview room. Before Jules could start questioning him again, the Professor said he wished to make a statement.

✧

16

W hen Jules entered the interview room Martin Samios was still trying to silence Professor Castleton, but he was determined to say his piece.

'Before we talk about Sarah Newhouse, I'd just like to remind you that you have no evidence whatsoever to prove that I was actually responsible for any of these deaths...'

'Apart from Christine Gleeson you mean?'

'Well yes...but all these other women already had something wrong with them when they came to me for help.'

'They didn't all exactly 'come to you'.

'Well I just happened to be there when they needed help. But they all had something wrong with them.'

Jules was trying to restrain her anger.

'I don't think Lily had something wrong with her - she was pregnant.'

The Professor clammed shut for a minute and Jules thought he was going to refuse to go on - but his ego got the better of him. Ignoring Jules's outburst, he re-composed himself.

'And now I'll tell you about Sarah Newhouse - another woman with something wrong with her who came to me.'

He took a sip of water.

'Sarah was a great believer in natural medicine. In the past I'd given her things for period pain, insomnia, lethargy. She was always happy with the results. There were never any side effects or near death experiences. But I hadn't spoken to her for about —-oh I don't know....maybe at least 18 months what with Covid and so on.....but now she was after me to give her something for some pretty serious menopause side effects. Mood swings, hot flushes - the lot.

I had told her to see her doctor about HRT. But apparently she had done just that but he wouldn't prescribe it to her because there was a history of blood clots in her family - and some other reasons - ovarian cancer I think. I'm not exactly certain what course of action he was recommending but she wasn't happy about it and several times she had asked me if I had anything that might help - which at that time I didn't really.

So life went on and I didn't hear from her for a couple of months - then about a week before she died, she phoned me and said things were getting worse and was there anything - anything I could do. She sounded pretty desperate. Anyway, as it turned out, since the last time I had spoken to her, I had actually carried out some trials of a new combination of plant hormones..'

'Were these official trials?'

'Not exactly, I was carrying out what I like to think of as 'pre-trials' where I get enough evidence to apply for permission to carry out controlled human trials.'

'Who were you pre-trialing these hormones on?'

'Not women - I wouldn't do that. You might be surprised to hear this detective - but it was Pigs! Pigs are excellent subjects to test for toxicity and so on. In many ways they are very much like humans.'

'Do you always test your medicines on pigs.?'

'No, this was the first time. I was concerned - especially after the allergic reaction that Miss Farmer had suffered - that perhaps there might be some unknown side effects I hadn't considered - although the plants used in Adele's medication were very different to the hormonal solutions I was working on now.'

'Did the pigs all survive?'

'One of them died. But I'd made adjustments to the mix since then...and pigs are sensitive creatures, sometimes they just can't cope with changes to their environment and have a heart attack and die. '

'Let's get back to Sarah.'

'Yes well we had a long discussion about her problem. I told her I had something that might work - but it was early days - at this stage purely experimental. But she was still willing to give it a try. You see - she came to me - I didn't force it on her. I told her it would have to be hush hush because I didn't yet have approval but she was fine with that. So I told her that we'd have to disguise the medication in case her husband saw it -because he didn't approve of natural remedies at all. So that day, I sent her out to buy some of those over the counter herbal menopause treatments. I stipulated that it had to be tablets in a bottle - not sealed in foil. She came back to my office that morning and I replaced the tablets with my own...'

'You make tablets?'

'Yes - I have an old apothecary tablet press - it works fine. - I collect antique medical equipment you know, although the tablet press is the only antique equipment I still use.'

He leaned across the table to Jules as if he was about to reveal critical information.

'Now this part is very important. I told her - very strictly - not to take the first dose until she got home in case it made her sleepy. And I stipulated - no - strongly insisted - that she was to stop taking it immediately and get back to me if it caused any unpleasant side effects. She promised me she would do just that and was very happy when she left my office that day. As far as I was concerned, she was going to drive straight back home to Cloncurry, and I left almost straight after to go looking for lime trees with Aunty Lydia.'

'Then what happened?'

'I had a very successful afternoon. We found the trees, I had a nice cuppa and a chat with Aunty Lydia and came back here to enter the field results. But when I came around the back, there was a car I didn't recognize parked in my space. It had dark tinted windows and I couldn't see inside, but when I went to investigate, there she was, slumped over the steering wheel, barely conscious. I could see the open bottle of tablets on the passenger seat so I knew immediately that she hadn't listened to me at all - and this was the end result.'

'Did you consider calling for help?'

'Well in this case I would have … probably should have - but I couldn't think of a way to keep myself out of it. To be truthful, I wasn't sure if she was getting worse, or if the effects would wear off. Her pulse was a bit fast, but apart from that she was just asleep. I tried to wake her but she'd just groan a bit and ignore me. I thought the best thing I could do would be to drive home and be seen there in case I needed an excuse. And if she woke up in the meantime or got worse- well I wasn't there any-way. So that's what I did - I went home.'

'But you didn't stay there.'

'No, after an hour or so, I thought I should check on her, so I rode back to the office on my bike. I didn't want my car to be seen there.

Unfortunately when I got back - she was worse - a lot worse. I could see this wasn't going to end well so I put on some PPE, loaded my bike into the back of her car - pushed her into the passenger's seat - and that wasn't easy - and drove out of town.

There had been heavy rain the day before which was a bit of a nuisance because it meant the ground all around the side of the road was a bit mushy. I had to look for somewhere private, but not too far off the road and not too far out of town. My bike wasn't fully charged you see, and I couldn't afford to get caught out. Finally I spotted a good location where the ground fell away - well you've seen it - and at that moment there was no traffic at all, so I quickly drove in there and parked behind that bushy area.

The next part was extremely hard for me. At one stage I thought I'd done my back in and that would have been a disaster.'

'What was so hard?'

"Firstly I had to pull her back into the driver's seat - and she's not a tiny woman. Then, when I unloaded my bike, instead of wheeling it away, I needed to carry it so any tyre prints wouldn't connect it straight to the car. At the same time, I had to watch out for on-coming traffic.

Anyway, I thought I finally had it all sorted, and was just about to strip off my PPE and leave when I heard her groan. When I went to check, her face was all contorted, she was barely breathing and her heart was racing. I thought - I can't leave her out here suffering like that - it might be hours before she died. Even worse - she might not die before she was found.

I was in a bit of a panic about what I could do, then I noticed there was a cricket bag in the back seat. I couldn't hit her with it while she was in the car, so I had to go to all the trouble of pulling her out again. That's when I put her out of her misery with the bat.'

'So you admit you killed her.'

'I'm certain she would have died anyway. I just didn't want her to suffer.'

'So you don't think she would have suffered when you hit her?'

'No it would have been quick.'

'So if you killed her outside the car, how come we found her in the car?"

'Yes I'm not sure why I bothered to put her back. There was no need. Just one of those things. There was a bit of traffic around too so it was quite reckless on my part. But at that time of the evening your eyes are on the road, so I took a chance that no one would look my way. For some reason I just thought that if it looked like she'd been killed in the car, I might be able to build a bit of confusion into the injuries. Honestly - I expected I'd be doing the autopsy anyway because I did the others. But getting her back into the car took a bit of time and by the end of it I was exhausted and there was quite a lot of blood. So I just stripped off all my protective gear and packed all the incriminating evidence - except for the bat - into my backpack. Then I rode off cross country for a while to avoid any witnesses. At one stage I saw a police car - probably the one that found her. By the time I got home I was completely exhausted. I had a shower and went straight to bed. Everything else you know.'

He leaned back in his chair and planted his hands on the desk.

'And that's all of them. One self defense. The rest - misadventure - or in the worst case - medical malpractice and inappropriate disposal of a body - which will be quite a punishment for me because it will mean the end of my career.'

'Well it was certainly the end of 5 women's lives.'

Professor Castleton seemed to noticeably perk up now that it was all over.

'But the important thing to bear in mind is - I'm not a murderer. And certainly not the serial killer some of the local newspapers have tried to make me out to be. I didn't go out with a knife or gun looking for victims, or have some kind of sexual perversion.'

'But the victims found you anyway.'

Nobody knew what to say, so after a short silence where everyone seemed to look down to avoid eye contact with each other, Jules wound up the interview and arranged for Professor Castleton to be returned to his cell.

Martin Samios explained that he would be applying for bail as the Professor was not a flight risk or a danger to others now that he'd been exposed. He also wanted a more complete psychiatric evaluation carried out.

'Still clinging to insanity as a defense are we Mr Samios? Well I'm certain it will come as no surprise to you that we will be opposing bail - but I'm certain we can get the trial underway pretty quickly. As for the psychiatric assessment, we will be happy to accommodate any experts you want to assess his mental state, but he sounds pretty sane to me - just lacking in any insight or remorse for what he has done. Anyway now that we've found Adele's car and Amy's luggage, we'll certainly be looking for more evidence. I'll keep you posted of course.'

"Pretty quickly" turned out to be an optimistic assessment by Jules Banyenan, although the Professor would be required to sit out the wait in prison. He was moved to Brisbane, ostensibly to be closer to his wife, who he had lived apart from for 23 years, although never divorced. Her first and only visit to him was to advise that she intended to divorce him and would not appear as a character witness under any circumstances. But plenty would. Over the next few months, several people, some prominent within the community - including Avery Jacks - came forward to offer support for his work and surprisingly - to admit that they had successfully sought relief for a variety of health issues from the Professor. Most of these issues were minor in the scheme of things - dodgy knees, headaches, rashes, chronic indigestion - but they all swore by his remedies, so much so that Jules was at one point concerned they might undermine her case.

He was also assessed by two independent forensic psychiatrists who both diagnosed him as a high functioning psychopath. Not a cruel killer who took pleasure in death, but someone only concerned with his own ambitions. He was, according to one report, 'convinced that what he was doing was for the greater good, even though he knew it was illegal.' They also noted his insistence on the use of the words 'quasi -illegal' to describe his actions, rather than the more accurate word, 'wrong.'

$\diamondsuit$

17

While the police prosecuting team was carefully assembling evidence, the now retired Senior Sergeant Jack Harding was slowly recovering. His bones had healed and he was now - gingerly on his feet again. His wife had arranged for them to move to a small unit close to the rehabilitation hospital where he spent much of his time learning how to walk again. He had two regular visitors. The recently promoted Senior Constable Nina Forde who kept him up to date with all the latest developments in the case, and, surprisingly, Joe Palmer.

For Nina and Jack, solving the case had been bittersweet. How many times had they listed Professor Castleton as a possible suspect? How many times had they dropped him off the list just as quickly because of who he was? How many clues did they miss that might have led them straight to him? They both agreed that the most serious error of judgment they made, was to be too quick to accept his version of events related to the death of Sarah Newhouse. That's where they should have pushed harder right from the start, especially when an unexplained toxic substance was found in her stomach. It might have at least saved the life of Christine Gleeson. But at the same time, both were excited to have been part of the team that solved the case. In particular, Nina Forde remembered the sheer relief she felt when she realized he was the one.

'I remember looking at Detective Inspector Banyenan and knowing she had realized it too. After all these years. It was an awesome moment. We were both trying to hold it in - the emotion - we didn't want him to know that we had him until we were ready to arrest him.'

'Why didn't Jules arrest him right then?'

'We had to get the charges right. Most of the evidence we had for the other cases was still circumstantial and if he knew we were onto him, there was always a chance he'd run. He has a lot of contacts overseas and dual citizenship, which is why he didn't get bail. We were lucky he'd been panicky enough to leave fingerprints behind at the cafe. Without those, we would have had to keep interviewing him and hope he made a mistake. We did have the tyre tracks from around Sarah's car that matched his bike - but they also matched a whole bunch of other bikes in the district -and that was about it. Adele had been cremated so there would have been no going back to her case for evidence. But Jules did consider applying to have Amy exhumed. In the end - thankfully it wasn't necessary.

In a way I'm pretty sure he was relieved it was all over. I think killing Chrissie had bothered him because he couldn't justify it to himself as some sort of medical misadventure. Even now he's still trying to claim it was self defense - though all he was defending was his reputation. It will be interesting to see how it all pans out in court, but finding the car and the luggage will help. The luggage in particular because they've found his prints on some of Amy's belongings in one of the bags.'

They both agreed that it was tragic that Jack had the accident when he did. Not just because he nearly lost his life and still had a long recovery ahead of him, but he had missed out on being in on the arrest after all the work he'd put in. Still, he would be called as a prosecution witness when Adele and Amy's cases were tried, which would give him some sense of satisfaction and closure.

Joe's visits had nothing to do with the case at all. He just thought Jack was a decent bloke and could do with some cheering up from someone who was not connected to the police. He would pop in with a box of fancy little cakes he'd picked up from the Hotel dining room and they'd sit and sip instant coffee and argue over how to solve the world's problems.

On one occasion Jack remembered the murder stone story and asked Joe about it again. Joe thought he had a copy of the book somewhere in his belongings and offered to bring it over for Jack to read. Jack wasn't up for that.

'Why don't you read it to me - you can explain it as you go.'

And so began Joe's regular visits with a tatty copy of a thin paperback that told of the travels of the legendary poet Matsuo Basho. The story that included the tale of the Murder Stone is really only a few pages long and could have been read in a single visit, but the philosophical discussions took longer than the story and it spread out over month. In the end the only things they agreed on was that the poet's love of nature and yearning to travel was somewhat akin to indigenous people's connection to important features within their own country - and that Jack would never learn to appreciate Haiku poems which he found too brief to have any meaning - and usually didn't rhyme at all.

By now, the slow dance of justice had begun but it was still one step forward and two steps back. The discovery of the suitcases and Adele's car had provided new opportunities to gather yet more evidence to test for prints, DNA and other foreign substances that might be connected to the Professor. Meanwhile, the defense gathered supporters and hoped they could reduce the impact of the Professor's confession.

Despite admitting to being involved in each woman's death, Professor Peter Castleton would not plead guilty to murdering anyone and the case would have to go to court. Jules thought it was a complete waste of resources given the evidence and the admissions made, but there were the finer points to argue about involuntary manslaughter and unintended consequences - and his team would try to discredit some of the circumstantial evidence on the basis that for at least two of the deaths, he wasn't actually present. For all his talk, the Professor had always claimed he was innocent of murder and Jules was determined to gather as much damning evidence as possible.

She phoned Nina Forde.

"I think we have to check out those pigs. The ones Millie mentioned....they came up during questioning and he said a couple were still alive - but where? Also we need to find maybe another laboratory somewhere - or at least another computer. There's nothing on the main computer we seized from his office other than regular pathology business and that little laptop of his only has maps and photos of plants and a few hundred botanical references. Nothing about elixirs or compounds or herbal mixtures. All that stuff has to be somewhere.'

'Did they search his home too?'

'Yep - His home computer had a lot of above board information about native plants. That's the one he was using to write his book and there were a number of research papers and so on there - and the guys are still going through that. But so far nothing incriminating - but he is fastidious with his notes and I'm certain he kept notes on all these deaths. Remember he did say he did some blood tests on Lily. Well where are those?'

'I'll get on to Millie and see if she can put me in touch with the boys.'

'OK - let me know if you need me to come up there to organize any special warrants.'

It took Millie almost two weeks to track down the two boys
who still lived in the area and get them to agree to talk to Nina.
She'd had to promise that everything was off the record, and
that if laws had been broken, they wouldn't face any consequences. Even then, Uncle Ernie and Uncle Charlie - (the two
elders who had put a stop to the pig hunting) insisted on being
present to protect the boys rights.

Nina and Millie met the two Uncles and the boys Isaac and
Eddy on a crossroads just outside of town. After Millie had
introduced Nina, she left. The Uncles invited Nina to sit with
them on a small patch of grass a little way off the road.

Uncle Ernie took the lead in the conversation.

'You want to know about the pigs?'

'Yes - and I want to know where they are now?'

'You give your word that the boys won't be in trouble?'

"I promise. '

The two elderly men exchanged a few quiet words with each
other in their local language and then nodded their permission
to Eddy.

'Ok Eddy - you tell the lady about the pigs.'

Eddy was clearly jittery about talking about the whole affair
but the Uncles stared him into talking.

'That professor bloke, he asked Issy and me and another
guy if we knew if there were any wild pigs around here. Yeah
we did. He said he needed them for research and he'd give us
$150 a pig if we could catch him at least 4. 5 would be even
better. Well that's a lot of money for something nobody wants
isn't it? I mean shooters go out and kill them all the time just
for nothing. Issy here - his brother had a ute so we said yeah -
that's good money. But we weren't allowed to kill them. He

gave us this dart gun and told us to use that so the pigs would just sleep. That freaked us out a bit - but then we thought - what's the difference? We're still just shooting them. The deal was - we'd ring him when we had a couple of pigs and he'd give us the address to take them too. It was just down there a bit and you turn left up a dirt road. Looks like a shed from the outside - but inside it's all new and stuff. The first weekend we got 2 and the next weekend another 3 - we got better with the dart gun. But one of them died on the way so we had to go out again and get another one.'

Throughout all this explanation Isaac - Issy - had sat silently looking down at the ground. Uncle Charlie gave him a nudge. "What have you got to say for yourself hey?'

Issy shrugged his shoulders but the Uncles weren't letting him off that easily.

"We didn't do nothing wrong. We just gave him the pigs. The first time, they were still asleep when we left. He just got us to help chain them up in these metal box things.'

'Cages?'

'Nah not cages - there was just bars between them and we chained them to the bar. It's a big place you know.'

'Can you take me there?'

Isaac looked at Eddy and then the Uncles. Eddy looked hesitant, but the Uncles nodded yes.

'Good - so when you got back with the other pigs, were the first 2 still there? '

'Yeah but they were pretty noisy. Squealing their heads off - you could hear them from way outside.'

Uncle Charlie butted in.

"When we heard that - we put an end to this pig business. It's not good to have animals screaming in pain like that. Not on our country. We went out there and told that Professor bloke to leave the boys alone. He reckoned he had a permit. Waved a bit of paper at me but I didn't get a chance to read what it really said.'

'Were the pigs still kicking off when you went there?'

'Nah, quiet as a mouse. Maybe all dead by then. Who knows.'

Nina stood up and brushed the dust from her pants. "OK - can we head out there now?' You lead the way.'

As they walked over to their SUV the boys mumbled something to the Uncles. Uncle Charlie turned to Nina. "The boys are not in any trouble - right?'

'How many times do I have to tell you - No. - In fact they might even be in line for a bit of reward money for helping us.'

At that news, they all grinned, got into the SUV and led the way to the Professor's shed.

To call it a shed was to totally underestimate it. Outside from a distance it looked like an extremely large but unimposing timber and corrugated iron barn - except that the roof was completely clad in solar panels

It was only as you got closer you could see it was more than a shed. At various points at the base and middle of the walls protruding pipes led directly into what appeared to be septic tanks sunk into the earth. A large air conditioning motor was mounted on the front left hand side of the building and there were two air vents at the back. There were no windows at all along the front or back of the building, but a whole bank of them down each side up high near the roofline. The kind of windows you normally see in a factory. And down one side were two big water tanks.

At the front of the building there was a solid, beige-painted wooden door, protected by a substantial security screen, while at the back sliding wooden barn doors protected an entrance big enough to drive a tractor into. All the doors were securely locked with keyless entry. Obviously no way to get in without a permit and no way to see in without a ladder.

Nina walked around the building with the boys, taking photos as she went. Eddy acted as her guide.

'Everything's very clean in there - like a hospital or something. There's two rooms up here at the front - we never went into them. I think they might be offices or something. See all them things on the roof? That's where he got all the electricity to run the place. Very clever aye?'

They walked around the back.

'The pigs were in here. Each pig had its own space- like a stall. There's also a big washroom thing along here. He could hose the pigs mess down. All the stuff came out here I think. (He motioned to one of the larger pipes). It didn't stink as much as I thought it would. Over there (he pointed towards the remains of an old shed) that's where we buried the pig that died on the way. He made us dig a pretty big hole so the dogs wouldn't dig it up.'

'Did you ever see anyone else out here?'

'No only him.'

Nina walked over to the waiting Uncles.

"Did you guys see inside when you came to see him?"

'No he spoke to us out here. He was wearing one of them suits - white - covered all of him, even his head. '

'OK well thankyou very much guys. I will record the help you have given me today and as I say, if he's found guilty of anything, you might be eligible for a bit of a reward. I'll be in touch.'

Nina sat in her car and sent through the photos to Jules, then drove back to the station to arrange a search warrant and get a forensics team together.

When Jules saw the photos she wanted to jump on a plane straight away and head out there, but she could see Nina and the team had it all under control. She'd just have to wait patiently for whatever they might find there.

The next day, warrant and break-in tools in hand, Nina and the team headed out to the Professor's shed. Forensics had recommended breaking in via the back barn doors where the pigs had been kept 'just in case there are carcasses there.' That way they'd be able to provide maximum ventilation.

There was a distinct whiff of 'pigs were here once,' but no sign of pigs recently. They checked out a large freezer, but nothing there either and clean as a whistle. One of the police suggested, 'Maybe he just let the pigs go when things started to look a bit dicey for him.'

Nina made a note that it was a question Jules could ask him.

As the boys had said, the place was pretty clean - especially the two rooms the boys had never been into. This was like walking into an undiscovered Egyptian tomb. The smaller room was clearly an office with a desktop computer and rows and rows of CD's and a drawer full of carefully cataloged memory sticks. The discs seemed to go back 21 years and covered topics such as *Ricinus communis experiments* and *Symptoms of Erythrina genus poisoning*, to *Results of Brugmansia spp as a treatment for depression*.

In a desk drawer were two phones that looked like pre-paid models. Very basic but both with sim cards removed.

The other room was even more revealing. This was his laboratory. A small fridge in the corner, kept working by the rooftop solar panels, was filled with various containers of plant samples, mysterious fluids and what looked like tissue samples. (Hopefully pig tissue). Along one wall were jars of preserved items - most dried, some preserved in fluid. Nothing had a name, but every container had a number - no doubt registered on one of the discs or memory sticks. The sheer quantity of evidence was enormous.

The forensics team put in a call for back-up. The room would need to be totally emptied.

To ensure there would be no room to appeal against any of the seized materials being submitted as evidence, Jules had kept Martin Samios fully informed of the search and committed to providing him with a list of seized materials. It would be a long list.

Once they had access to the computer, they found file after file of people identified only by letters or numbers, who had taken part in the Professor's experiments over many years. All were ranked with stars - like you might rank a hotel or a restaurant. The more stars the better - but no stars didn't necessarily mean death. It just meant failure. The commentary around the stars indicated that most was hearsay or anecdotal rather than scientific which was strange for a pathologist as highly qualified and experienced as the Professor. It was as though he had one set of values for conventional medicine and an entirely different set of values for native plants.

A brief interview with him clarified the pigs issue. One had died and been butchered and dumped in one of the septic tanks. The others had proven to be too troublesome to be reliable test animals and so they were set free. It was his understanding that one of the freed pigs had later been hit and killed by a passing truck. And yes, all the tissue samples were from the pig who had died. We could throw them out because he didn't need them anymore. The forensics team wouldn't do that of course, not before ascertaining for themselves that they really were all pig samples.

18

Months dragged on while the Professor's legal team sought to delay the inevitable, but finally a date was set for the trial to begin. It was now March and the date was set for September. There was still work to be done on all the material and files from the Professor's laboratory, but none seemed critical to the first case to be tried, so there was no reason for the prosecution to delay. Given how long the Professor had already been in jail, Martin Samios managed to get a judge to agree to him being released on strict bail conditions that included him reporting to his local police station twice a week and handing in both his English and Australian passports.

Jack had made good progress and was now up and about and walking with the aid of a walker. He was confident he would have recovered enough by September to travel to Brisbane for the trial, if needed. In the meantime, he would go through all of his files and search for anything that might help strengthen the case even further. Copies of everything had been sent to Jules and after a few months of nothing new to report, he was about to pack up his files when a note fell out with Danny Banda's phone number on it. He remembered that just before the accident, Danny had agreed to take him up to the back area of the park where he believed Christine Gleeson had destroyed an extensive area of native yams. His accident had put paid to that, and what with the arrest of the Professor and all his physio sessions, he had totally forgotten all about it. Now he toyed with the idea of calling Danny to arrange it - but there seemed to be no point. By now it had been a good few years since she had been up there if at all -and whatever she had done would have grown over and have no bearing on the case. Besides, as his psychologist said, it was important for him to let go of things. But Jules no longer sent regular emails asking after his progress and Nina Forde rarely visited - (but did at least phone every couple of weeks to see how he was going). Even Joe seemed to have disappeared. He needed to find something else to occupy his time. One thing he knew he did have to do, was face up to the demons that were still waking him most nights. He needed to return to the place where he almost lost his life and see that it was just a place, not a nightmare.

It was an unseasonably warm day when Jack climbed into his SUV and headed down the Barkly Highway to Cloncurry. He stopped at the police station to catch up with some old mates who told him that 'yes, Danny Banda's still the head ranger out there,' then headed out of town to the park. He told them he was hoping to see Danny and thank him personally for helping to save his life. Thinking about it, he was embarrassed he hadn't done that already - although his wife certainly had on more than one occasion - and so had the police. He decided he would explain to Danny that he wanted to come out to his land to say thankyou in person - rather than just call - and that it was only now that he was well enough to drive long distances.

So that's exactly what he said when he found Danny at the rangers office. Danny was gracious enough to accept his thanks without asking what had taken him so long and Jack was offered a seat to rest his legs.

Over a cup of tea, Danny recounted what he'd witnessed that day and how he was pretty certain that Jack was a goner. He thought Jack looked pretty good for a guy who had to be cut out of a car with something called the Jaws of Life. 'Big bugger of a can opener thing. Pulled the car apart.'

Jack thanked him again and got up to leave. Danny held the door open for him.

'If you still want to go up and look at the place the woman dug up, give me a call. I could do it next week if your legs are up to it.'

'Sure - why not. I'll give you a call.'

Then he left, walked around the spot where his life nearly ended for a few minutes and drove - very carefully - back to Mt Isa.

All the way back to Mt Isa, Jack thought about whether there was any point in taking up Danny's offer. The only possible reason he could think of, was if the actual site was significant for some reason. If maybe it was another place Chrissie could have seen the Professor on his bike - otherwise it was just going to be a case of ecological vandalism in the name of culinary progress. But he hadn't spent much time in the park at all, so it would be interesting to get out in the fresh air, take a look around, and have another chat with Danny - to get his take on things. When he got home he called and arranged to meet up again the following Wednesday.

Meanwhile back in Brisbane the prosecution had initially planned to join the death of Amy Moreno and that of Christine Gleeson to the same indictment on the basis that the murder of one was linked to the murder of the other. But after much debate it was decided that getting a straightforward murder conviction for Christine Gleeson would make it easier to prosecute the other cases which were not as clear cut. Being forced to accept his guilt might even make the Professor agree to plead guilty to a range of charges for each of the other victims, saving the court time and money and making it easier for the families of the victims. One thing was for certain, the prosecution team did not want to provide grounds for an appeal under any circumstances. They had continued gathering evidence as they tested each part of the Professors story and now besides the fingerprints left behind at Christine Gleesons' cafe, they found the Professor's prints on the inside rim of one of the buried suitcases belonging to Amy Moreno, along with his DNA on the discarded PPE which had been shoved into one of the bags.

In the case of Adele Farmer however, they were less successful. In an open suitcase in the boot of the car, were the remains of clothes and shoes, but between the fire, exposure to the elements over many years and a recent flood, there was no forensic material of any use. All they could be certain of is that the shoes and clothing belonged to Adele Farmer and that the car had been hired by her. As for Lily Fernandez, if the Professor changed his mind about his involvement in her death, they would have nothing to link him to her - unless Cheryl Hinkler could remember anything more - and that was not very likely. Despite a new search, they hadn't even managed to find the jack he supposedly discarded out there.

The following Wednesday Jack packed a thermos into a small daypack and loaded up two walking sticks and set off to meet Danny Banda. He'd packed sticks instead of a walker because he couldn't imagine the walker wheels would handle the terrain very well. He needn't have worried either way, the actual spot that Danny had been talking about was no more than 200 meters off a fire trail and over fairly flat and accessible open ground.

Jack couldn't figure out how Chrissie would have known to come here in the first place, but Danny believed he knew why.

'It has some of the best areas of wild yams and other herbs around. I reckon she probably heard about it from one of the Aunties. Look at it - it's remote, but easy to get into and out of because of the fire tracks. Very few tourists come up this far, so she could take her time and no one would see her unless they just happened to be coming this way. I didn't even see her up here - just in other parts of the park. It was only when I came up here to make sure the tracks were still clear that I found this whole area around here had been destroyed. Course it's all grown back now. But you can still see where it had been dug - quite deep too. I think she dug the yams out instead of just pulling them up. At the time when I found it, she'd tried to smooth it all over - make it look like nothing had happened here. But I could see what had been going on. '

Jack walked around the site trying to see what Danny saw. Right now it just looked like a healthy patch of vegetation - minus the yams.

'What made you so sure it was her?'

'She was the only one who ever came up this way to collect stuff. She had a permit. No one else had a permit to do that. '

Danny pointed out the area that still showed where the damage had been done. "Look here, that area there is all sunken. I've been up here after a heavy rain and it drains straight away - no puddles at all, whereas around here (he pointed to an area nearby) the water sits on the surface after a downpour. She's disturbed the whole balance of the area. And the yams have never come back as strong. Just mostly grass and weeds now.'

Jack looked closely at the sunken area. 'Do you think she might have buried something there?'

'Buried? What would she bury?'

'I dunno. But it kinda looks like something's been buried there. Have you got a shovel? Can we dig up around this patch here?'

'No....no..we're not digging up anything just so you can poke around. It's already been destroyed once.'

'What if you got permission from the elders?'

"Why would they give permission? No, forget about it. I just wanted you to see why I was so upset with her. Anyway you got the man now, we can leave this land in peace.'

'Yeah, you're right. We got the man.'

The two men sat down on the grass and shared the contents of Jack's thermos while Danny pointed out the features of the landscape and how each part related to the other. After an hour or so, Jack decided it was time to go.

Something was bugging Jack all the way home but he couldn't put his finger on it. Never mind, as Danny said, 'we've got the man now'.

A week before the trial began, Jack paid a visit to the Cloncurry police to wish them well at the upcoming trial. Several officers, as well the butcher Geoff Baxter would be giving evidence. For all of them, it was an exciting if horrific prospect - something unlikely to be repeated in their lifetime. Jack agreed.

'The most serious crimes I'd ever had out here were some assaults, a few fatal accidents and one or two missing persons who eventually turned up after a few days.'

Sergeant Chan thought for a moment.

'No, we've had another unsolved mystery around here. Goes back to before I was here but I remember reading the files. Two indigenous girls - can't remember their names - just disappeared. There was a big search at the time but nothing was ever found. '

Jack wracked his memory.

'.........That's right. We were asked to help out. Wasn't there drugs or something involved?'

"Hmm, I'd have to check the file again - but I think that was the general opinion everyone had at the time, although whether there was any truth to it……. For a while there was also talk of a white girl missing with them too. That's in the file. But no young white girls had been reported missing and no one saw any unknown girl around here at the time. The two local girls were supposed to be pretty wild. My feeling at the time, reading through the file, was that they just took off somewhere. At least that's what I hoped…. though I remember when you found that skeleton…'

'Lily Fernandez..'

'Yes Lily…when you found her we passed on details of the two missing girls in case she was one of them. But of course…….'

Jack said his goodbyes and climbed into his car. Now the thing that had been bugging about the yam site loomed large. He called Danny.

'Danny - is it possible that those two girls that went missing a few years ago are buried in that yam place?'

There was silence from Danny, then - 'Do you think that's possible?'

'Well they've never been found. Can you remember, did the digging take place around the time the girls disappeared?'

'I'd have to think about that……maybe…. but they searched all around here for them girls. Up every fire track - the whole place. Dogs here and everything, so the digging must have been after. I'd say at least a few months after, when everything had quietened down and gotten back to normal. I remember we closed the park off while we were searching for the girls. Nah, couldn't be. I think you're barking up the wrong tree.'

'Well maybe, but can I ask you to talk to the elders about giving permission to dig the place, just to put everyone's mind at rest.'

'Can't you do a test or something to see if there are bodies buried there?'

'You mean with radar or cadaver dogs or something?'

'Yeah - something like that.'

'Honestly, it would be quicker if we just got permission and took a couple of shovels up there and dug a small section. We'd soon have a yes or no and then we could call in the specialists.'

Danny reluctantly agreed to talk with the custodians about the dig and get back to him.

It was day 1 of the trial when Jack finally heard back from Danny. It was agreed that Jack and Danny would be permitted to supervise the digging up of a small area of yams but that only men appointed by the tribal elders would carry out the actual dig. Now that they had said yes, the elders were insisting it would need to be done straight away so people wouldn't have time to think about things and get upset all over again. They wanted the dig to take place the next day because the families wanted the answers now. Fortunately Jack was not required at court and could - with a bit of reshuffling of his commitments - make it down to the park the next day. He was happy to let someone else do the digging, because he still wasn't up to anything that demanding.

When he arrived at the site, hobbling on his walking sticks, he found the families of the missing girls huddled together on the very edge of the yam patch and several young men marking out a patch in the center under the direction of Danny.

'Good morning Jack - do you agree this is where we want to dig?'

'Perfect - right where it dips there. Now we need to be careful here. We want to scrape the soil away just in case something is just under the surface - understand?'

Danny had already rolled out a tarpaulin to the side and reminded them that all soil removed needed to be placed on the tarp, where it could be carefully sifted and placed back into the hole when they'd finished. Then they began to dig.

About 50cm or so below the surface a small piece of clear plastic appeared. Everyone stopped for a moment and took a deep breath. From over to the side, wailing began. Softly at first, then uncontrolled.

Now the digging team threw away their shovels and used their hands to expose more and more of the plastic. By now enough had been revealed to confirm the worst. There was at least one body there, the remains of feet barely visible through the badly discolored plastic. Jack immediately stopped the dig against everybody's wishes.

'Okay, Okay…I know you want to know who it is, but we have to do the right thing here. There are people who can handle this with respect and care - protecting the body or bodies and any forensic material. We need to keep in mind that it's not just about knowing who is buried here - but who did the burying.'

The families nodded their agreement.

Jack looked over at the team of diggers.

'What we need to do now, is cover this site with the tarpaulin - including all the earth that has been dug out - and call the police. I know it's going to be hard for you all, but we are all just going to have to be patient while the experts take care of it. It's been many years now - so a few days more is all I'm asking for.'

The families of the two missing girls had already decided they knew who was under the plastic and were inconsolable, but they agreed with Jack. The important thing now, was to find out who put them there.

While Danny went back to his office to organize some tarpaulins, Jack called Cloncurry Police and told them what they had found, and to ask them to organize a forensics team immediately. In the meantime he also wanted them to station a guard at the site to ensure no one interfered with anything before the forensics team arrived. They readily agreed even though Jack had no authority to give anyone any orders. Danny Banda and Jack stayed to wait for the police, but everybody else was encouraged to leave. The families seemed glued to the spot, but Danny promised them they could come back tomorrow and wait for the bodies to be exhumed. That seemed to satisfy them somewhat and they drifted off home.

In Brisbane meanwhile, the trial was progressing as expected. The prosecution was using the Professor's claim of self defense against him. Defending your reputation was a strong motive for murder. The jury must have been totally baffled. The crime scene photos shown in evidence didn't help his cause. Why not leave after the whack across the back of the head? Why then reach for a second weapon to attack her with when she was already badly - if not fatally injured? No one expected the trial to last long - it was just going to be a matter of whether he was found guilty of murder or manslaughter. Jules knew it was important to get a murder conviction now, to set up the case against the Professor for Sarah's death. These two cases were definitely the prosecution's strongest. Despite new evidence, there was still a real chance that involuntary manslaughter would be the final outcome for the cases involving Adele, Amy and especially Lily.

By day three of the trial, the prosecution case was complete and Jules was feeling a lot more relaxed about the outcome. As she left the courtroom, she turned her phone back on to check for missed calls. At the top of the list was a message from Jack Harding. "Could you call me when you get a chance.'

Below that, was a message from Detective Tom Anthony of Mt Isa police. "There's something I need to speak to you about - urgently.'

She called Jack first. He was pleased to hear from her.

'How's the trial going?'

'Good - I think everything's under control.'

'Glad to hear it.'

'Jack - I've got a message to contact Inspector Tom Anthony at Mt Isa urgently - do you know what he wants to speak to me about?'

'Yes - about that. Look, I asked him to speak directly to you about this because we - or should I say the police - haven't completed the investigation at the site yet - but we've found another body - well maybe two bodies. I think it might be those two young girls that went missing. '

Jules felt her legs go wobbly under her. 'What?'

'We won't know until tomorrow when the forensics team comes out but - well - it could be linked to your case in some way.'

'How?'

'Danny Banda thinks Christine Gleeson was involved. That's why I was up there looking around in the first place. Well if she was, that could have an effect on whether the jury thinks of her as a victim - or a dangerous woman capable of killing.......but look, it's still a lot of 'ifs' right now. Even if it is the girls, it doesn't mean she put them there. Danny just blamed her for digging up yams, not burying bodies. '

'Jees...I'd better call Tom Anthony. Good work Jack.'

As she hung up, she realized her hands were shaking. What the hell was going on here? First things first - she'd call Tom Anthony.

'Tom I've already spoken briefly to Jack Harding. What's going on here?'

'Honestly, I don't know. I haven't been up to the site yet - I'll head up there tomorrow with the forensics team. But from what I understand, the Chief Ranger up there…'

'Danny Banda,'

'Yes, that's the man - he'd mentioned to Jack just before he'd had his accident that an area of ground had been dug up and he reckoned Christine Gleeson was the guilty party. Anyway apparently Jack was going to check it out at the time - but after the accident and his retirement and so on he forgot all about it. Then a few weeks ago, he took Danny up on his offer to go up there and take a look. According to Jack, it looked to him like someone or something was buried there - but he had to get permission to explore it further. I think in the end the elders agreed because there was a couple of girls that went missing a few years ago. Do you know anything about that?'

"It came up during our investigations but there was nothing to suggest it was connected to these other deaths. I believe there was a comprehensive search at the time and nothing was found.'

'Well I wasn't around then either and the inquiry was run out of Cloncurry so it's all new to me. I thought you should know in case it has some effect on the trial.'

'I'll mention it to the DOP of course, but I can't see why. The Professor has never raised the issue - and I'm sure if he suspected she was involved in burying anyone up there he would have used it as part of his self defense story…so…but look, as soon as you know anything - anything at all, let me know.'

The DOP as it turned out was concerned about the effect it might have on the case. Right now they didn't know who was buried there - or by whom. Certainly no proof it was Christine Gleeson who'd done the burying, but probably wise to have a meeting with the judge to talk it through - and perhaps suggest a delay until they had at least established how many bodies were buried there - and who they were.

The judge saw no reason to delay the case, as this was a trial involving only one victim - Christine Gleeson. If it turned out upon further investigation that she had also committed a crime, so be it. At no stage during his defense so far, had the Professor's team suggested that Christine Gleeson was a violent person given to making physical threats, therefore it had no bearing on the matter. The trial would go on. If further information came to light, the situation could be reevaluated.

By the time the forensics team turned up at the dig site, the families of the girls had set up camp a respectful distance away to keep watch. They'd been there since dawn and were already performing a ceremony for the dead - even if it wasn't their dead. Jack had bought his own camp chair and an esky full of food and drinks. He was there for the long haul. Detective Tom Anthony came over and introduced himself to Jack and the families before moving closer to the action. Only Danny was not there. He had been at first, but the whole episode bothered him and he left after speaking to the families. It made Tom Anthony a bit suspicious at first until Jack reminded him that the site was only discovered with the help of Danny.

'It's more likely that he feels guilty for not recognizing it as a burial site- or at least investigating it a bit more thoroughly than he did.'

The exhumation was a slow process - the forensics team didn't want to miss anything from the badly decomposed site.

Even so, they were less than an hour into the dig when they realized they were looking at more than one body. By lunchtime it was obvious there were more than two. By mid afternoon, the third body had been removed. The first two were wrapped in clear plastic, side by side. The third, buried deeper and probably placed in the hole first - wrapped in black garbage bags. Despite decomposition, it was obvious they were looking at the bodies of three young women. All still completely clothed. From the color of the hair, one other fact was obvious. One of the women was blond - probably bleached blond - but blond all the same. The other two had dark hair. The forensics team had a conversation with Tom Anthony. He now had the difficult task of talking to the families.

He told them that there were three women buried there - but that unfortunately it appeared that two of them were likely to be their daughters.

The mothers immediately wanted to look at the remains, to confirm they belonged to their daughters.

'That's not a good idea. They've been there a long time - so there's really not much left to recognize.- but they were buried in their clothes and we might find other belongings too. Jewelry, purse, phone - that sort of thing. Why don't I arrange to have photos taken of the remains of their clothes - and you can identify them that way.'

The families were too upset to respond but it kept them away from the remains for now. Inspector Anthony shook the hand of one of the elders, expressed his deepest sympathy and walked away. There was a lot to be done.

Carefully each body in its wrapping was placed into a black opaque bag and carried into the back of a van to be driven away. The forensic team stayed behind to sift through the displaced soil looking for anything that could identify the bodies or the person who had buried them there. One by one, every-one else drifted away, leaving only two forensic officers, plus Jack and Inspector Anthony. The inspector had sent two mes-sages to Jules during the day. The first said, 'Three bodies - two almost certainly the two missing indigenous girls. The third likely caucasian.' The second message said, 'Initial observation suggests no blunt force trauma to the head of any of them.'

Later in the day, he called her. 'There's no obvious signs of violence to any of the girls. The caucasian girl who is still unidentified is a complete mystery. She may well be as much as 10 years older than the others, although they're pretty sure she hasn't given birth. The other girls have been identified by their clothing. One of them was wearing a fairly distinctive studded jacket. Even without DNA proof I'd say it's definitely them. But as for the other girl...well, she was always just a rumor according to the local police. They weren't ever looking for a third girl. I can't even find anything in the files about the first person who mentioned her. - Oh and the other important piece of information - apparently at the time the girls went missing, this whole area was locked off and searched with dogs and everything. So they were either still alive for some time after they disappeared - or hidden somewhere else for a few weeks before being buried here.'

'OK. Well let me know as soon as the pathologist has some-thing useful to tell us. Have you found anything that's going to help with the identification of the other girl?"

'Not at this stage. We're already onto missing persons in Brisbane. There are no missing persons reports outstanding for anyone that fits her description from around here. The team is still searching the gravesite for information too. We might find something there but we might have to rely on dental records for this one. No one seems to have missed her.'

This crime scene was starting to look more and more like the story that had woven itself around the girl's disappearance right from the beginning. That is, that the girls had been victims of some sort of drug deal gone wrong. Nothing to do with the Professor and probably nothing to do with Christine Gleeson either. She'd always denied she had dug up the area and she was probably telling the truth. Mind you, the soil was pretty soft around there. Wouldn't have taken a lot of effort to dig and the bodies weren't buried that deeply. Finding out who the third girl is might clarify the situation.

$\diamondsuit$

19

After just 1 hour of deliberation, the jury came back with a guilty verdict. They hadn't bought the idea that the Professor felt physically threatened. It's not like Chrissie was holding a gun or a knife. But the key evidence was the pathologists report that she had her back to her killer when the first blow was struck. And, she was facing into a food storage area, not leaning across a kitchen bench reaching for a knife or some other weapon. Much to his horror, the Professor was sent back to his cell to await sentencing. The judge had a lot to take into consideration. Not just his motivation and mindset but reports from both forensic psychiatrists and a number of character references suggesting he was not by nature a violent man and had done a lot of good for a great many people.

His legal team knew this was just the beginning of a very long process. Yes, they could work on grounds for an appeal, but waiting in the wings were all the other charges relating to the deaths of Lily Fernandez, Adele Farmer, Amy Moreno and Sarah Newhouse. They already knew that the death of Sarah Newhouse would be next, because there was evidence she was still alive when the Professor attacked her with the cricket bat. And they had toxicological evidence of a substance present in her stomach contents that matched substances later found in the Professor's private laboratory. It would be one thing to say the poisoning was unintentional, and quite another to explain away why he felt the need to attack her with the bat. And that would be before they even got into the discussion about why he didn't seek help for her in the first place.

At Police Headquarters meanwhile, the good news of the guilty verdict was tempered by the knowledge that every person sitting in jail as a result of tests carried out by Professor Castleton, would now be challenging that evidence. The mess his conviction would create could take years to clean up.

✦

20

Two days later, just as Jules was heading into work, she received a call from Jack Harding. He sounded concerned, not even bothering with his usual greeting.

'Hey Jules - this call is strictly between you and me, yeah?...'

'Sure Jack, what is it?'

'One of the girls - when they unwrapped her and removed her clothes, they found a phone - a phone!....and it's in pretty good nick. It was in one of those plastic covers and appeared to have been shoved down the back pocket of jeans she was wearing. Anyway the team in forensics are pretty certain they'll be able to find out when it was last used - who she was in regular contact with. The killer must have missed it because every other personal item has been removed. There's no wallets or jewelry or anything to identify any of them. Nothing on any of the bodies except their clothes. Could be a real breakthrough. They've already shown it to one of the girl's mothers on the quiet and she says it looks like her daughter's phone. When Tom Anthony calls - don't let on that I told you. I'm not supposed to know.'

Shortly after, Tom did indeed call. Jules acted surprised and excited to get the news.

'I assume you've tried to charge it - is it working?'

'Sort of - takes a bit of a charge and stops. We think the battery is cactus - we're onto a replacement to see if it will fire up. The SIM card's not looking too flash though - but we've identified the provider and we're just waiting to hear back from them. To be honest, I'm a bit surprised their phone records weren't examined when they went missing - but I guess that fits with most people thinking they'd just run off.'

'Any closer to identifying the caucasian girl?

'We do have two possible matches from the national database. One from Darwin, the other from Byron Bay of all places. We're trying for dental matches - her teeth were well cared for by the look of things so we're hopeful. The forensic pathologist also can't find any signs of long term neglect on her skeleton. No signs of ongoing violence. Nothing you'd expect to see if she'd been living on the streets or anything like that. '

'Is there a chance she was from overseas? A backpacker or something?'

'Possible I guess, but her clothes and shoes were all brands readily available here. I'm beginning to form the idea that she may have been used to lure the girls with drugs..or there could have been a sex angle to it...she could have come through here with one of the truckies."

'Only problem with that Tom - is that whoever buried these girls up there knows the area very well. They have to be a local. Not someone passing through.'

'Well maybe we have to take another look at the Ranger bloke - he was acting very strange when we were digging up the bodies. Just took off without a word. Didn't want to know who was buried there, or how many. I know Jack doesn't think he's good for it, but he knew the girls and knows the area better than anyone.'

'No..I think I agree with Jack on this one. Even when Jack had completely forgotten about the offer to check out the area - Danny reminded him. Not something you're likely to do if you've buried bodies up there. Jack thinks he just feels ashamed that he didn't recognize there were bodies buried there and I think I'm with him on that. When I look at the photos taken before the dig, it's pretty clear that something was going on. He would have been able to tell something's not right. I just don't know why he didn't report it to anyone.'

'So maybe Christine Gleeson was involved after all.'

"Possibly…but I think if Danny thought she was involved he would have had no hesitation in coming forward. No love lost there. But look, who knows at this stage? Let's just wait and see what that phone tells us. I want to know who the girls were talking to before they were killed. But I also want to know if there's any way to track down signs of poisoning. And I want to know if the plastic is the same type that was used to wrap Lily Fernandez.'

"Whoa - that's going to a whole different place.'

'Yes I know - but it's a place we know exists, so it seems logical to me that it's something we should explore. Anyway the Professor's not going anywhere so let's see what we can find out from the phone first. '

'Onto it.'

He hung up.

Between a new battery, some miraculous rescuing of data from the sim card and a helpful telco, the phone gave up its story.

The last income calls were all from her mother and an ex-boyfriend. There were at least 20 of them, all unanswered and cluttering up her mailbox with variations of 'where are you?' ranging from extremely anxious to outright angry. Half way through the last message, the mailbox registered as 'full' and the phone went dead.

The last outgoing calls were made almost 4 hours before all the incoming calls.

Two were made within 15 minutes of each other to a number listed as belonging to Cecily. The number was attached to an unregistered prepaid phone which no longer responded. There was a good chance Cecily was the unknown third victim, although neither of the missing girls they knew about was called Cecily.

There was a call to a local truck driver who had coincidentally died in a house fire a day or two after the girls disappeared, and one to a friend who was over an hour away in Mt Isa when the call was made.

An 'unknown' number was also called three times in succession. The calls had all been answered, with conversations ranging from 30 seconds to 2 minutes and 57 seconds. That phone number was listed as belonging to a Dr Peter Castleton.

On the day those calls were made, Professor Castleton was staying at the Muttaburra Motel in Cloncurry. He'd driven down to collect fresh plant specimens for a series of zoom lectures he was due to give to a conference in Switzerland. His topic was **'The Life and Death Power of plants.'**

On hearing that the police wanted to talk to him about the recently unearthed bodies, the Professor's demeanor immediately changed. He would say nothing more except to deny everything. But he knew we knew.

It was over.

A weathered skeleton
In windy fields of memory
Piercing like a knife

Basho

✧
About the Author

P.K. Kaplan spent many years working in advertising writing television and print commercials where you always had to stick to the truth.

One day, while relaxing in a bath at her home in Melbourne she decided to set her imagination free and write a murder mystery.

Her interest in Japanese literature and First Nations culture is central to the narrative of The Murder Stone, her first published novel.

P.K. Kaplan.

www.ingramcontent.com/pod-product-compliance
Lightning Source LLC
Chambersburg PA
CBHW052111030426
42335CB00025B/2939